butterflies on a sea wind

# butterflies

## on a

## sea wind

BEGINNING ZEN

anne rudloe

**Andrews McMeel**
**Publishing**

Kansas City

02 03 04 05 06 MLT 10 9 8 7 6 5 4 3 2 1

ISBN: 0-7407-2721-4

Library of Congress Control Number: 2002103673

Book design by Holly Camerlinck

## Attention: Schools and Businesses

To Dae Soen Sa Nim, Bobby, and
all the other teachers at PZC
and elsewhere

Zen Master Hyang Eom said, "It is like a man

up a tree who is hanging from a branch by

his teeth—his hands cannot grasp a bough, his feet

cannot touch the tree—he is tied and bound.

Another man under the tree asks him, 'Why did Bod-

hidharma come to China?' [Bodhidharma was the

Indian monk who came to China and founded the

Zen tradition.] If he does not answer, he evades his

duty and will be killed. If he answers, he loses his life.

If you are in the tree, how can you stay alive?"

# First Retreat

Zen practice is quite different from any worldly
study. All the knowledge and learning that you
received before should be discarded. You should
give up thinking that you are doing something
now. Your mind should be blank; you should
again be like a one-year-old baby.

ZEN MASTER PUYONG

I drove up and down the same stretch of rural mountain road six times, looking for a dirt trail near a garbage Dumpster that the directions said would lead to the retreat center. When I finally found the path and started up the North Carolina mountainside, the trail switched back on itself in impossible turns and ruts that the car strained to get past. Finally it opened into a level meadow with several new wooden buildings and a garden. The mountain rose up in forested silence above the little settlement.

When we were called into the meditation hall at dusk, there were two rows of flat, square mats stretched in long lines on the polished hardwood floor on either side of an altar. Two people in long, gray robes sat on either side of the candlelit altar. The last evening light glimmered in the windows, and cicadas sang in the summer night outside as some twenty people in t-shirts and sweatpants filed into the huge, open room and sat down on the mats.

After everybody was settled, one of the two leaders got up, stood before the altar, lit incense, extinguished the candles, and sat down again. The scene was wonderfully exotic! After years of reading about Zen, I'd finally found it in the flesh.

I perched kneeling on a thick, round cushion that I'd upended on the mat. My legs were tingling and rapidly turning numb but, since everybody else sat motionless, I did too. Bit by bit my legs turned to lead, and it took looking to see if my feet were still part of my body.

Little itches began to pop up at odd spots, first on my nose, then between my shoulders. Wasn't anybody else uncomfortable? How could just sitting still be so hard?

After what seemed like forever, the sharp crack of sticks hit together three times ended the sitting period. We were told to remain silent for the rest of the weekend and sent to bed. My legs had no feeling whatsoever. I unfolded them slowly—it felt like manipulating remote-control robot arms—and toddled off to the dormitory. The retreat would begin at 4:30 the next morning.

A marine biologist by profession, I helped run an aquarium and marine environmental center in Florida. A tiny, independent, non-profit organization, it barely managed to stay open. My husband, Jack, and I periodically ventured into the office buildings of New York or Washington to scrounge up a book contract or a freelance magazine assignment. An academic scientist by training and inclination, I taught part-time at a nearby university and had received occasional research grants. Despite the professional difficulties of our rural location, neither of us wanted to leave the forest or the sea.

It was the uncertainty of this lifestyle that had reawakened my long dormant interest in this spiritual tradition. I'd first encountered Zen years before in college and immediately knew it was one of the most important things I'd ever found. But it seemed premature for a twenty-one-year-old to focus on the difficulties of life when I'd hardly even lived yet. Twenty-five years later, in middle age, I was ready to explore it. Maybe practicing Zen would help shift attention from my endless personal wants and frustrations to the vast and beautiful world around me.

The next morning we all began our long day of sitting in silent stillness on the cushions, watching as morning light revealed a round, stained-glass flower in the wall high above the altar. The point, we were told, was to be aware of each moment just as it is, just the room as it was at that instant.

Participating in a retreat is not about sitting all tied up in knots worried about personal issues, nor is it about waiting for a cloud of enlightenment to descend upon one's head. A Zen retreat is very simple. We were just there to experience being still if possible and to see what can arise from that stillness. The main goal of the effort is to quiet the mind of discursive, analytical thinking and allow it to express itself in different ways.

Analytical thinking is important; we can't get through life without it. Analysis has led to the great advances in our understanding of the physical world that we call science. Rational analysis is one of the most wonderful aspects of human reality, but it is not the *only* way the mind can function. In meditation, we pause and learn to allow the intuitive pathways we've neglected and forgotten to open as well.

A teacher is present to provide a little advice on how to proceed. There's nothing more than that to a retreat, nothing to get out of it except that opening experience. A retreat allows us to simply experience how life is when we're not busy hustling and grasping and being judgmental.

At first sitting was peaceful, but pretty soon my legs started to hurt again, and we weren't supposed to move or make any noise. The longer I sat the more insistent the throbbing was until finally I had to move my leg out a little, trying to be as silent as I could. Then my nose started to itch—was I supposed not to scratch it? About the time I couldn't stand it any longer, the leader signaled us to form a line and start walking around the room. We got ten minutes of relief, but then we had to sit down again. Hours of this lay ahead. None of the many books I'd read about Zen philosophy or history had prepared me for the reality of this situation.

One at a time, we left the room for a private interview with the teacher. Each of us was new at this. As we walked to the interview room, we had no idea what to expect. At least it was a chance to get up, move, and talk to somebody. I could sit and stare at the floor all day long at home anytime, I thought irritably.

When it was my turn, I entered the room and sat down on one of the square mats and round cushions on the floor directly opposite the teacher. Wanting to make a good impression and show off in some vague way, I had an opening speech all ready.

"Good morning, how are you?" the teacher said.

"Fine, thank you."

"Do you have any questions?"

"Yes, I do. Ten thousand times I come to this interview, ten thousand times you ask me a question, ten thousand times I answer wrong, and yet still you sit here!"

There was a pause.

"So what?" the teacher said.

"So what? So what! So, how do you do it?"

"The sky is blue, the grass is green."

The teacher leaned back, waiting for my response, but I didn't have one. I tried again.

"I want to learn about Zen, but it's hard because there is no teacher where I live."

"The best teacher is within—there's the true teacher," he answered, gently poking my belly with a three-foot-long polished wooden stick, and laughed.

"Let me ask you a question," he added. "What is Reality?"

"The Tao?" I responded, referring to the Chinese philosophical system that describes a dynamic, aware energy in everything.

"That's just a word—what does it mean? Show it to me!"

Show it? Being there was like being Alice in Wonderland. Nothing made any sense in this strange conversation, and pretty soon I was back in the meditation room.

An hour later, sore muscles weren't the only problem. I was bored to death. Each minute seemed to last for an hour. What was this all about? Tempting though it was to leave, that would be too embarrassing. For years I had read books about Zen and wanted to try it but had no idea where to begin. Only after a friend had handed me a brochure for this retreat center had I known whom to contact. I couldn't give up so quickly.

But even in the midst of an increasingly angry and critical mental commentary, I couldn't help but notice the sunlight gleaming on the polished oak floors and the bright colors of the mats and the altar. In its simplicity and openness, the room did have a certain aesthetic quality that was new and different.

But then sleepiness became overwhelming. Why did we have to get up so damned early anyway? Asking us to rise at 4:30 A.M. and then sit still and alert all day was like breaking somebody's ankle and then telling that person to enjoy the scenery during a hike through the woods.

Beginning a meditation practice isn't easy. When we start, backs ache, legs go to sleep, the nose itches, boredom and restlessness reverberate off the walls. If we don't flee at this point, however, the mind begins casting about, desperately looking for input. We try to focus as we were taught and pay attention to the breath for a while. However, when we've had enough of that, we're still stuck here anyway.

After a while the mind may start a refrain of I can't do this, why should I anyway? It's good for somebody else but it's not my style; it's Oriental claptrap and mystical mumbo jumbo. That's just a mental speech that everybody makes sooner or later, a speech that's usually associated with aversion, pain, and boredom. The legs and knees hurt, a headache comes from lack of sleep or caffeine, and suppressed emotions begin to surface. But there are pragmatic reasons for doing all these practices; there's nothing mystical about them. The techniques have been preserved for thousands of years because they work. If you practice long enough and sincerely enough, insights will inevitably arise. Life will become richer and more vibrant.

In order to get to that point, however, the body as well as the mind has to be physically trained. One usually sits cross-legged on a square mat with a small cushion under the hips to support the back. Until the thigh muscles are stretched out enough to allow the knees to rest on the floor, this can be an awkward position to hold for a prolonged period. Once we get used to it, though, it's the most balanced position for remaining still for a long time. If sitting that way is physically impossible, sitting in a straight-backed chair is okay. The hands are placed one on top of the other, and held just below the navel. Allowing them to rest on one's legs creates more strain on the lower back.

The back, neck, and head are held straight—slumping makes breathing more difficult. The eyes should be kept open but focused on the floor at about a forty-five-degree angle in front of the body. Closing the eyes makes it easier to become drowsy or for the mind to wander.

If the knees or back hurt, notice how the mind spins around with thoughts like This hurts. This pain is bad. How can I escape it? But if I move I'll fail in front of everybody and be embarrassed. Watch the pain. What is it really? What does the intellectual abstraction, the word, actually include? It's a series of sensations that arise and change constantly, passing from one form to another, sometimes disappearing, sometimes not. Is it pressure, is it tightness or tingling? How does the sensation change? What mental state does it generate—aversion, fear, what? How does that change? Watch the show inside your head for a little while. Then adjust your posture.

This phase is also a time to learn to pay close attention to your surroundings. Since nothing obvious is going on, in the endless quest for relief from boredom, we see more and more minutely. We perceive subtle things happening. Even in the midst of the mental grumbling, the mind begins to notice things that were lost or beneath notice in the course of daily life. The way the light changes in the room from morning to night, or all the nuances of crunchiness and texture in eating an apple suddenly appear. We may also begin to notice the way the mind works, how it hops randomly around, trying to find a way back to the routines it's used to.

Just as the body must become more or less stable, the thinking, analytical mind must come to rest for the duration of the meditation period. That's not easy either. The mind is unruly. It's like a wild colt that's never been trained to carry a rider, or a little puppy that we order to sit still. A puppy mind sits for a half a second, and then it's off and racing around again, remembering the past or speculating about the future, reviewing its agenda of goals or opinions. The puppy seems to want to be anywhere except quietly sitting on the cushion.

Focusing on watching one's breathing is the traditional way to keep the mind from wandering all over the map. Watch the breath as it expands the abdomen or as it passes in and out of the nostrils. Count each breath from one to ten, and then start counting again. If the mind wanders, go back to the count of one immediately. It can take a very long time to be able to reach ten without having to start again.

If watching the breath isn't enough to stop the mind from chattering to itself, repeat a mantra. A short phrase such as "What is this?" on the inhalation, "Don't know!" on the exhalation, a mantra is like a radio jamming frequency that blocks discursive thoughts. There are many such phrases—the actual words don't matter that much. You could repeat "Coca-Cola, Coca-Cola" if that worked best for you.

When the mind wanders, it's pointless to get angry or frustrated. Just patiently and peacefully bring it back one more time to the breath. When thoughts arise, just notice them and let them go, always coming back again and again to the breath. When emotions arise, simply be aware of them too. Emotions filter and color everything else that happens. Watch how they do that. If anger or frustration develops and the teacher says something to the group, those comments will be a personal affront. If you feel happy, you wonder why everybody else seems so grim. Don't they understand anything?, you wonder from your height of superiority. In several days of sitting, emotional states will shift like a kaleidoscope. Nothing will be forever, and that's a major lesson.

After the silent lunch, there was a break, but I couldn't relax and go to sleep. I gave up trying and went for a walk on the mountainside. A little way along the path, a blue wildflower blazed in the sun with a clarity and intensity that most flowers don't have. As I squatted and stared at it, a single mosquito flew past at eye level, and then a spider appeared hanging on a thread of silk in midair, shining in the afternoon light. As I moved slowly and silently, everything was somehow sharper and clearer than usual—like a photographic image suddenly coming into focus.

By that night I was so tired and stiff I could hardly sit down on the mat again. A silver and crystal mesh of cricket and cicada sounds sparkled in the black night under the stars, but reality, however defined, seemed far from clear. And when in the name of anything holy would this day be over?

By the end of the weekend, I was so sore from the long hours of sitting that I could hardly walk. The teacher's comments still didn't make much sense. But driving down out of the mountains to the flat Georgia plains, headed home to Florida, I wanted more of this elegant, rigorous practice.

# Why Zen?

Those who seek liberation use their personal
existence as the furnace, the Dharma as
the fire, wisdom as the smith.

BODHIDHARMA

Many of us today are over-stretched, trying to balance too many things. We all want to be happy, but too often happiness is out there, somewhere over the horizon, something we'll get to in the future. When things don't work out in accordance with our desires, we move on, change partners, change jobs, or trade in whatever isn't right for a better model. It's always easier to keep moving than to stop and face the fundamental questions: Who am I? What is really happening here?

Spiritual practice is the quest to answer these questions. It is both the highest adventure that life offers and the most intimate of all human activities. A journey through all the nooks and crannies of the human experience, spiritual inquiry is the effort to connect with a larger reality, to master the self and its endless puzzles and boundaries. It's the never-ending asking, What is this? What's the point? Why am I here? that won't go away or be ignored.

Zen practice is a powerful method of spiritual exploration. Even though Zen originated in Asian monasteries over a thousand years ago, this spiritual path is still relevant today. It can help us maintain a viable balance between our personal needs, career obligations, and the deep-seated need to understand our role in a vast and starry universe.

Zen is based not on faith in any revealed truth or dogma but in the direct, immediate experience of our own lives. Zen means to sit with an open heart, asking, Who am I? What am I?

Since Zen is a path of personal discovery rather than a set of dogmatic beliefs or answers, its meditation techniques can be and often are adapted for use by people of various faiths. Whether we are Christians, Buddhists, Jews, agnostics, or anything else, the techniques of Zen practice can be used to deepen our spiritual awareness.

In Zen meditation, we learn to be still and allow the neglected intuitive forms of consciousness to operate. To do that, we first learn to pay attention, to be fully present in each moment and aware of the nuances of life. It takes a while, but every bit of improvement in this skill is a wonderful gift we give ourselves each day. And it's done by relaxing, not by forcing. When it doesn't have a specific job, we let the mind rest quietly rather than chatter compulsively to itself, endlessly raking through its collection of possessions, desires, likes and dislikes, plans and memories. Achieving that quiet mind isn't quick or easy. The mind dearly loves to talk to itself.

Nevertheless, if we persist, this practice can dissolve our ignorance and the confusion and pain that ignorance inevitably brings. And once all that is gone, then happiness and peace are simply there. We begin to live with more clarity and to act with more compassion toward all our fellow beings. In time, the clarity may get a little worn and frayed, so then we come back to the meditation hall and work under retreat conditions to restore it.

Like science, Zen practice is a way of trying to comprehend the larger reality that exists beyond our personal affairs. Unlike science, however, Zen is equally concerned with human affairs, does not try to divorce the humanity of the observer from the rest of the universe being observed. It focuses precisely on the relationship of the individual to everything else, asks the question What is a human being's job in this vast and starry universe?

Beginning Zen practice as a layperson through a series of small retreats interspersed with affairs of work and family is the path most American Zen students encounter. Most of us will not do the long years of intensive practice necessary to become a Zen master. However, we can use the powerful techniques of Zen practice to make our lives more whole and sacred and to find our Way in the midst of our daily lives.

The centuries-old monastic practices of Zen are designed to realize the intense focus and energy that is inherent in each of us. We preserve and use these techniques in formal retreats. But meditation is not some kind of self-centered spiritual hobby. What to do with what we have learned in retreats will come to us after we have come home again. We learn to bring the focused attention that we've practiced in retreats to other activities in our lives. Instead of the traditional monastic lifestyle, the circumstances of our own lives provide the raw material for spiritual growth.

Beginning a Zen practice can be a sink-or-swim business. Books on Zen philosophy don't often give much indication of what it's actually like to sit down on a meditation cushion and start to practice. Reading about Buddhist or Zen philosophy divorced from *practicing* is a recent Western innovation. For the first time in the long history of the Zen tradition, teachings are widely available in print, and large numbers of people are literate and can study them privately. This is a huge shift from previous generations, when serious, in-depth teaching was always included in the context of intensive meditation retreats and monastic practice.

While this shift makes these concepts much more widely available than they ever were before, there is also a need to be careful. It's beneficial to read, study, and discuss ideas and philosophy, but if that's all one does, it's rather like reading the label on a medicine bottle and debating what it says but never taking the medicine. Serious Zen includes meditation, formal practice in a group setting, and engagements with a deeply realized and experienced teacher who can see and challenge all of the ego's endless protective games and encourage the student to maintain a deeply questioning mind of humility and openness.

Yet in the West today it is very common for people to refuse to consider the possibility that there could be anything gained by studying with a teacher or using traditional techniques in developing a spiritual practice. Many people read books about Zen, but only a few actually practice in a rigorous setting, and almost nobody trusts a teacher enough to work with him or her long term, in a one-on-one relationship.

There are several possible reasons for such reluctance. Modern Western culture is extraordinarily individualistic. Perhaps we fear the intimacy required in a relationship with a spiritual mentor. Sometimes our egos can be affronted by the idea that we can learn anything from anybody else on such a personal matter, or at the idea that our personal situation could be in any way similar to someone else's. People may distrust their ability to distinguish a true teacher from the hordes of self-serving spiritual hustlers who are unquestionably out there. We may respect academic or scientific credentials and expertise because we have some understanding of what those credentials mean. However, we may distrust spiritual credentials because we don't understand what they represent in terms of training.

Nevertheless, after doing some reading, we may finally decide to sign up for an Zen retreat. There, more often than not, the rationale for the methods used is not explained, and a group of strangers sitting in silence may seem intimidating and unwelcoming. The schedule may be exhausting, and it may seem impossible to survive the day. In addition, traditional Zen teachings, which come from a monastic tradition, often have little to say about the primary issues most of us face today, such as earning a living and raising a family. It's not surprising that many beginners give up in confusion and frustration.

Despite the steep learning curve at the beginning, it is worthwhile to keep trying. Sometimes a moment of clarity and spiritual awareness arises in the midst of daily living, unexpectedly shimmering like a spring flowing deep in the forest. Compared with that, formal Zen practice is rather like drilling a well. It finds water too, but it works slowly, painfully, and requires enormous effort and commitment. But those springs rarely appear spontaneously for most of us. If we want to reach the water, maybe we'd better start drilling.

Staring at that silence and stillness long enough, merging with it, we eventually come to realize that the answers to our questions are within that stillness. We don't penetrate the silence, it penetrates and dissolves us. Once that experience begins to occur, continued practice widens and deepens it. We practice because our lives are beginning to work better. We realize that everything is our teacher, if we just pay attention. And we discover that there is no conclusion to Zen practice.

# THREE

# Down Home Zen

There is nothing to appear before you, and
nothing that is lost. Even if there were
something it would all be names, words,
phrases, medicines to apply to the ills of little
children to placate them, words dealing
with mere surface matters.

ZEN MASTER RINZAI

$B$ack in Florida after the retreat, the aquarium, as always, seemed a bit lost in time. Old wooden buildings with casually landscaped wisteria and azaleas housed a collection of seawater tanks and aquariums. Water bubbled and flowed in a swirl that sustained our collections of the bizarre and the beautiful. Unlike most big public aquariums, which house porpoises and large fish, we focused on sea horses, hermit crabs, emerald-eyed spiny boxfish, electric rays, and red-and-white-spotted calico crabs—all the endless living treasure of a still shining coast. Over the years the place had grown from a research supply facility into an environmental education center. On weekdays school buses unloaded excited kids who discovered that the world was bigger than they'd ever dreamed.

One morning while waiting for a school bus to arrive, I wandered in to look at the seawater trays. Water bubbled through the filters. Sea horses hid in the seaweed, their black and bronze heads dusted with gold flecks. Starfish moved effortlessly over the sand, and the octopus was out of its burrow. Red hermit crabs with bright blue eyes carried waving sea anemones on their shells. Together with animals that looked like plants and plants unlike any on land, they challenge our concepts of what it means to be an animal, of what it means to be alive.

Is this really okay, what we do here? I asked myself for the thousandth time. We kept everything alive, but sooner or later some of these animals would be shipped to universities all over the country. Few would ever swim in the open ocean again.

These animals had helped increase people's awareness of the diversity and beauty of living beings. Some had contributed to the discovery of new drugs against cancer, but none were here of their own volition. Lowly invertebrates that lacked friendly eyes, brains, soft fur, or feathers, they were still as fully alive as any cute mammal. Was it really okay to use them in these ways? Did doing this fit the Buddhist concept of right livelihood? Was this a way of earning a living that created no suffering or harm to others?

Yes! I finally decided, standing there waiting. It's okay. In collecting marine animals along the shore and bringing them back to the aquarium, we were still hunter-gatherers depending on the bounty of the sea to survive. And hunter-gathering was the niche humans evolved to fill, the way humans originally lived.

Hunters lived intimately with their environment, cultivating a sense of the sacred as a natural expression of their dependence and appreciation. Nowadays, the goal of our hunting and gathering was to bring others into contact with the living world so that they'd better appreciate a little of the ancient reality within which all humans once lived. The fact that our hunting and gathering was now embedded in a complex technological system of jet planes and universities didn't change the fundamental reality of this way of life.

In fact this life of collecting marine life, running an aquarium, teaching kids, and supporting the work of other scientists not only was okay, but was a gift and was essential to the environmental activist work I did. There are so very few left today who still follow the ancient and honorable way of the hunter-gatherers. The development of agriculture contributed to some of the problems of humanity being out of balance with our planet, such as too many people, huge disparities of wealth, and maybe even large-scale genocidal war instead of tribal raids. Agriculture and the population surplus it had created, myself included, were what threatened the planet's environmental future, not subsistence hunting and gathering, I concluded triumphantly. Unlike most Buddhists in the agricultural civilizations of the modern world, I was some sort of Pleistocene Stone Age Buddhist, still out there hunting and gathering.

When the bus arrived and the children poured into the aquarium, I immediately noticed one particular kid. He was overweight and had a slightly unusual face. He looked very unhappy, and I watched him as I ran through the introduction. He was clearly disliked by the other children, who rebuffed his efforts to gain their attention all during the tour. When I gave him a little extra attention, he responded eagerly.

If only kids would love one another instead of isolating and being cruel to those who are in any way different, I thought. If only humans could love one another a little more. However, this matter of rejecting those who are different is hardwired—it might even go back to tribal survival in the Pleistocene, when a nonconformist was considered dangerous to the group's survival. Countless scholarly studies of socially isolated children have been published by psychologists, and they all boil down to the basic fact that kids reject anybody who doesn't fit in their peer group. And, for that matter, so do adults. To transcend this persistent cruelty might require another, more insightful species of human. Today, an exceptional few highly motivated and trained spiritual practitioners achieve minds of great love and compassion and are recognized as saints. Any of us—if we put in the lifetime effort—could attain and express that mind, but most of us just don't make the effort.

After the noisy busload of children drove away, I took off to a salt marsh across the bay to plan a slightly different field trip for a university ecology class on the following weekend. A Gulf Coast salt marsh is neither of the land nor of the water—it has its own reality. The pine islands, forested, slightly higher ground surrounded by intertidal grassland, looked like ships at anchor in the sea of grass. Beyond, the marsh opened up into a tan prairie stretching away forever. Smaller pine hammocks sat on the distant horizon, blue-gray, giant Pleistocene mammoths, grazing scattered across an ancient landscape, motionless in eternity. They crouched on the horizon like mythic self-aware beasts, as a river of wind and cloud flowed overhead, enormous energy sweeping effortlessly past. Carrying fall butterflies and shining silken grass seeds, this wind had blown for millions of years, long enough for the plants to discover how to ride it.

A storm had pushed the sea up hard against the land, and the marsh was flooded with six inches of water, covering the salt flats, shining under the dense stands of needlerush marsh. It had rained all night, and another storm was coming. It was not the best weather for such scouting, but time was running out.

I waded farther out to the edge of a tidal creek. It looked pretty deep. If we got here near high tide, we wouldn't have to carry the canoes too far. We could probably do a three-hour trip and still get back before the tide drained out again.

In spite of the weather, some butterflies were out. The flamboyant monarch and sulfur butterflies that had poured through in their October mass migrations were almost gone. But a few strays remained, moving exclamation points of orange and yellow intensity on the brown land. They fed from the tiny blue sea lavender and white aster flowers hidden under the needlerush. They moved about with great purpose and determination, these stragglers who had stayed behind here as each migration passed through. The die was cast; they somehow had made a choice to remain and gamble on a warm winter rather than face the perils their fellows who traveled on would risk to avoid winter altogether. Or did they have a choice?

The immediate purpose of the trip was settled, so I turned back toward the wall of forest behind the marsh. It looked like a shoreline in its own right, with coves and headlands of trees washed by the sea of grass. The rain fell harder than ever. White sand, clear water, streaks of marsh grass, and streaks of rain—each drop hit with a white flash of light, and the water surface shimmered from the vibrations of the impacts.

When asked by a visitor to write the essence of practice, Zen Master Ikkyo simply wrote, "Attention." When pressed for more, he wrote "Attention, attention, attention!" Frustrated, the visitor asked what *attention* means, and Ikkyo said, "Attention means attention."

In paying such attention to a salt marsh, what might there be to discover? The rain moved back in with a vengeance. The tree islands on the horizon floated in a layer of mist, only their crowns visible, surreal against a sky that moved in and out on fragments of wind. Forgetting the rain, I sat down on a log. The interplay of light and water danced and danced. It had something to say, but I couldn't make out what. Maybe it had something to do with "the sky is blue, the grass is green." But I couldn't really sit and soak in the slow rhythms of the place in a way that would make it clear. I would have to come back when there was enough time. And somehow I would have to know how much time was enough. A few hours, weeks, a lifetime of seeing?

Several months later I was out on the bay beyond the marsh. Limestone rock outcrops lay scattered across the sandy bottom like oases in a desert, their surfaces coated with yellow, red, and lavender sponges and sea squirts and soft corals. Unlike a desert, the sandy, open areas were also full of life, but most of what lived in them was small and hidden beneath the surface. Whatever fish were present had darted away as I dove into the water. The green, murky water was itself alive, full of innumerable microscopic plants and animals, too small for me to see individually.

Sea whips covered the rocks like a forest. About two feet high, they looked a lot like bare-branched trees in winter except that they were bright yellow, purple, or orange. Their branches were encased in a white fuzz of feeding tentacles, which captured microscopic food out of the current as the tide rose.

The longer I looked at them, the more there was to see. Tiny, skeleton-shaped, shrimplike creatures hung on to the sea whip branches, bending and flexing as they too seized food that was too small for me to see. Little snails, members of a species that occurs only on this particular sea whip, were barely visible, perfectly matched in color with the sea whips. The snails' color came from what they ate, and they ate the sea whips' surface tissue. Yellow sea whips had yellow snails, purple sea whips had purple ones.

Zen practice emphasizes staying aware of each moment as we live it. If I hadn't already known about the snails and looked carefully, I never would have noticed them. The world is full of subtleties, and a lot of the time we are so preoccupied with our personal agendas, reviewing the past or anticipating some future moment, that we overlook most of what is before us in the present.

A cynic once observed, "We can't imagine that there is nothing more to life than just the experience of the moments between birth and death. That would be too absurd! Our existence . . . must have some greater meaning, and if the universe won't tell us what it is, then we will have to make something up."

Watching the tiny shrimp and snails on the sea whips, I realized that those moments between birth and death are exactly what we have in life. If we just pay full attention to each of them as we live it, the universe will tell us what it's about. And I strongly suspected that it was as much about sea whips and snails as it was about humans.

# Second Retreat

The more you talk about It and the more you
think about It, the further from It you go;
stop talking, stop thinking and there is nothing
you will not understand.

ZEN MASTER SENG-TS-AN

In the midst of field trips and feeding the sharks, images from the Zen retreat stayed in my mind. Eventually I located some other people in the local area who were interested in practicing Zen. About a year after that first retreat in the mountains, the newly formed Cypress Tree Zen Group organized a retreat and found enough paying customers to bring down a teacher from the Northeast.

This second weekend retreat wasn't at a lovely mountain meditation center. It was in a day-care center where we hung sheets over the walls in a vain attempt to cover up the ABCs and Mickey Mouse figures. The air was stuffy in spite of the roaring, rattling air conditioners. The rug under our sitting mats was hopelessly stained and faded from years of small children and their accidents. Trucks roared up and down the busy highway outside the building every few minutes. I cringed at the prospect of two days shut up in this place.

The schedule was exactly what it had been at the mountain retreat. All day the routine went on, sitting and walking in circles and sitting again afterward. My mind was anything but still, and I doggedly recited, "What is this? Don't know!" Repeating this mantra was like using a bit to control an unwilling horse. Nothing much in the way of insight was likely to appear at this rate.

At a formal retreat, everything is done according to a schedule that allows very little free time and challenges everyone from before dawn to late at night. The discipline and silence of a retreat are walls against which the individual's personality bounces, reacting sometimes positively, sometimes negatively. Some parts of the experience we like, but other parts of it seem awful or ridiculous.

Normally we try to avoid what we don't like. However, in a retreat, if we stay, we begin to see how our mental reactions actually make things harder or easier. The process highlights how opinionated and self-centered we are in familiar activities and how much we like to stay in comfortable routines. We resent being corrected as we make mistakes in learning the apparently arbitrary rules, and then we see how easily our egos are affronted.

Maintaining silence in a retreat cuts out using talk as entertainment. Talk is a way to pass the time without confronting the depths of our non-understanding. Silence also reduces our tendency to judge and rank everyone we meet, deletes all the internal gossip that supports our own egos and tendency to be judgmental.

For a beginner, the long day may be physically and mentally grueling. However, it is training to develop the courage, patience, and willpower necessary to do what is required in any situation regardless of whether it is difficult or easy, or what personal likes or dislikes arise in dealing with it. This training teaches us how to cope with major life crises—cancer, death of a loved one—the unpleasant things that are absolutely unavoidable.

Those who sit without aching legs, who radiate energy while beginners are floundering, are not superbeings and saints. They're just people who are stubborn enough to persevere through the initial stages of getting used to the physical demands and beginning to get the mind focused. A sitter has to be patient and steady. Trust will be sustained by the direct experience of what begins to happen—food is delicious, colors bright, the world vast and beautiful—then the effort is clearly worth the initial struggle.

To persevere at Zen practice requires faith—not faith in an external deity but faith that it's really worth the effort it takes and that these methods can bring us more clarity in life. It also demands a great question—the absolute need to know what life is about. And it demands great courage—the strength to persevere through the rocky spots.

Practice and experience, the teacher explained at a talk halfway through the morning, is what this Zen approach was based on—not faith in external authority. In the Kalama Sutra, the Buddha commented,

> Do not believe in anything simply because you have heard it. Do not believe in traditions because they have been handed down for generations. Do not believe in anything because it is spoken and rumored by many. Do not believe in anything simply because it is written in your religious book. Do not believe in anything merely on the authority of your teachers and elders. But after observation and analysis, when you find that anything agrees with reason and is conducive to the good and benefit of one and all, then accept it and live up to it.

It sounded like something Ben Franklin might have said. No wonder Americans liked Zen.

"The goal is freedom," he continued. "When we're free, we have the strength to do whatever is needed in each moment but at the same time, we're always playing, dancing in the sunshine."

While the goal might be freedom, the reality of that moment was that I was bored out of my mind. Time dragged without the normal busywork of life and without talking. It became clearer and clearer how thinking really does stop awareness, since I couldn't seem to stop thinking all weekend.

"Smile as you walk," the teacher suggested, but my immediate response was to think, When a smile comes, *then* I'll smile. A few minutes later, "Keep your eyes down on the floor" rang across the still room.

My eyes were firmly fixed on a tree outside the window since I was trying to focus on it as some kind of natural teacher. I angrily refused to lower them. Was this response coming from inner certainty or was it just ego asserting itself? What was the difference?

Traditional rigorous Zen practice induces suffering from lack of sleep, the long hours of meditation, and facing one's emotional issues, but it does so in the same way that a doctor sometimes causes suffering. It is only to help heal the underlying disease. Participating in a Zen retreat is like sharpening a pencil. In order to get it to a sharp point, you have to grind it down a little. Without the edge of struggle, the requisite strength to face life fully and courageously will not be developed.

After choosing a path, it's important to stay with that path, and not turn away as it starts to challenge us beyond our comfort zone. Serious spiritual practice in any tradition will eventually strip us of every self-protective attitude we have. If we endlessly play the spiritual tourist, superficially participating in many styles of practice but never going deeply into any one of them, we will never attain the resolution we seek.

After lunch there was a question-and-answer session, a blessed relief from the silent sitting.

"What about eating meat?" somebody asked.

"You eat meat, it's not important. You don't eat meat—also not important. What's important is why you eat what you eat," the teacher responded.

"Are people so different from other species when all life on the planet eats life?" I asked, thinking about the endless living and dying in the ocean.

"Yes," he said. "People have love and people have compassion. This quality is unique to people. Animals don't have it, so how can you practice love and compassion if you kill and eat meat, even though all other animals do? Not eating meat is a step toward practicing love and compassion.

"And humans are more complicated," he added. "A cloud appears in the sky when conditions are right for it to appear. It reflects light, releases rain, holds heat, then it dissolves back into the air. It doesn't try to leave a personal mark on the sky or to make the sky better as a result of its momentary, transient existence.

"Humans are not really different from the cloud," he continued. "We appear out of something, we function for a while, then we disappear again. Unlike a cloud, however, many of us want to feel that our individual life has meaning and that the world will be better for our having lived.

"In the course of human history, we have moved from hunting to farming and cities, to the current appearance of computers and space travel. This cultural growth doesn't just float down out of the clouds. Everyone contributes to these changes with every daily interaction in the work we do—whether it's raising the next generation, growing the food we need to survive, working to resolve disputes that arise, or treating sickness. These activities hold societies together and are just as fundamental to the human journey as making the next major scientific discovery or writing the next great piece of music that will be played for generations to come. Our religions have changed as well. They have grown from the propitiation of whimsical spirits in order to survive, to ideas of good and evil and justice, to ideas of love and compassion and finally the experience of self-transcendence."

He bowed, concluding the talk, and we all went back into the silence. But not all the meditation at the retreat was silent. Pounding spoons, wooden blocks, and rattles, we marched in a line in circles and spirals, chanting Buddhist sutras every morning and evening.

A traditional meditation practice, chanting sutras probably originated as a means of preserving the early records of the Buddhist tradition in the centuries before they were written down. The sutras are records of events in the history of Buddhism and interpretations of practice compiled by many authors in many times and places. Unlike the Bible, sutras are not usually claimed to be creations of divinity. Those describing the life of the Buddha were written down only after five hundred years of oral transmission, and many that claim to be records of his life are clearly written by later authors. But even after the oral teachings were committed to writing, the tradition of chanting was continued for its power in focusing the mind.

Chanting is probably the oldest form of human prayer, a song of thanksgiving and unity with all of creation. People have been chanting in nearly all cultures ever since we became human. An army of noisy, happy lunatics—clatter, clatter, tock, tock—led by one calm monk, we marched in circles and the Buddha was dancing on the altar.

What a way to earn a living! This guy was a Zen master, so he must be enlightened. I guessed he probably knew what he was doing. Zen master. The title had a fine ring to it. Do Zen masters have no more problems? I wondered. Do they always know what to do? Are they happy all the time? How do you get to be one? His teaching seemed to combine demonstrating the correct way to behave in whatever circumstances arose and, during interviews, nudging the students in some way closer to perceiving directly what can't be explained rationally. It looked a lot different from the university lecture style teaching I was used to.

Beginners often assume that Zen, like nearly everything else, involves working toward a goal, getting some new attainment or possession. In this system the goal seems to be something called Enlightenment, realizing the ultimate truth of everything. The details are a bit hazy, but it looks like a humdinger whatever it is.

However, looking for a spiritual thrill or thinking that we might get to be somebody special or that we won't have any more problems to face misses the point. A spiritual experience is like any other experience—it doesn't last, and after it's finished life is still there to be dealt with. Attaining personal Enlightenment can be just another self-centered desire. Realizing and then doing what's needed in life is what's important.

At 4:30 the next morning the gong rang to get up, and doing what was needed, getting up, wasn't welcome at all. Nevertheless, if I couldn't make this effort now, how would I ever be able to give what's really asked in life? Some roosters in a chicken coop behind the day-care center were crowing as they had throughout their history—ten million years, twenty million years?

How long have roosters been crowing? How long have people been making this sort of effort? I wondered groggily, rummaging for a toothbrush. Does this training really go back to Paleolithic shaman training thirty thousand years ago, fifty thousand years ago?

Religious belief and experience is one of the oldest manifestations of human reality. If such activity is so fundamental, does it hint at a

function of human self-awareness in this universe? Religious awareness and the compassion that arises from it—is that what we are supposed to be about? I wondered in front of the sink. Maybe human
self-awareness and religious beliefs are nothing more than haphazard
by-products of big brains and neural complexity, but for some reason
I had a growing conviction that the universe is alive and that we are
part of it in some meaningful way.

Outside, the peace of the world seemed closest to the surface in
the predawn. By day peace resubmerges under all our various affairs
and thoughts, like the ocean plankton coming to the surface at night,
resubmerging by day. When I came inside for formal sitting, the walls
and electric lights seemed like barriers.

All day, I tried to focus more on doing the practice correctly, on
trusting the methods and really doing them consciously. The empha-
sis on sitting still was obviously necessary to enable people to experience silent solitude in a group setting with a teacher, but sitting
totally still was also stilling the body, and that had to happen before
we could still the mind.

After a while, life began to seem like a series of still photos, each
one arising and dissolving into the next. An endless series of these
transitory moments, rather than the seamless flow of time we usually
take for granted, dominated my awareness. And for the first time a
glimpse arose of one of the basics of Zen: directly experiencing the
truth of impermanence.

Everything we cling to for security and think of as permanent is
actually a flux in time and space. We may understand impermanence
as an intellectual abstraction, an idea, but we never experience its
physical reality until we sit down on the meditation cushion. To go
beyond our usual dependence on relationships, possessions, and

accomplishments that are sure to pass, to live fully and in joy even in the midst of day-to-day difficulties, becomes easier when we look into the nature of our mental processes in a quiet, nonanalytical way and directly perceive the flux of our impermanent situations.

If all things—possessions, status, accomplishments, relation-ships—are impermanent, then endlessly seeking, receiving, and los-ing them is simply not the way to fulfillment for more than a second. When we directly experience the ever-shifting nature of reality for the first time, we may become less grasping and the suffering that comes from our desires can begin to fade a little.

This altered sense of time and impermanence was an eerie and fascinating experience, but it lasted only until my back started to hurt. Then practice consisted of paying attention to the physical dis-comfort—not enduring it, not trying to avoid it, just paying atten-tion, seeing how it came and went, appeared and dissolved. Doing that wasn't easy, but it also wasn't impossible.

In developing a meditation practice, there are several broad stages through which people tend to move. The beginning is often difficult because there are all the traditional hindrances of doubt, aversion, desire, and so forth to be worked through. There is also the need to get the body physically in shape and to become comfortable with the forms of practice. We must decide whether we really want to explore this spiritual path enough to deal with the obstacles. All in all, it's a process that can't be hurried. What make staying with the effort possible are the positive things that arise simultaneously, such as a greater awareness of beauty and the momentary relaxation of our fearfulness.

When we get used to the situation, "thinking meditation" arises. A little peace and quiet in which to sort out personal issues is a very rare thing, especially in the overcommitted, noisy lives many of us lead. So we use this quiet time to sort through the issues in our lives and situations in great detail. We may begin to recognize recurrent emotional and thought patterns as clues to something deeper rather than just being swept along by them.

As we explore our mental closets, a lot of understanding of the specific issues we're looking at may arise. We can take this understanding home and put it to use so that Zen practice becomes a do-it-yourself therapy. Or the situation may get so emotionally painful that we slam the door and leave.

Even though it's not really the point of Zen meditation, this introspection may be a necessary step for many of us. In the first few years of practice, we may work through a lot of unresolved personal business, and when we're finished the meditation that was so rich becomes flat, boring. Nothing is happening, so why continue? The job seems to be done. However, that point is the real starting gate. Instead of obsessing about personal problems we can begin to explore the nature of the mind itself.

With the clarity and attentiveness that eventually develop from long-term meditation practice, we can start to move toward an understanding of reality that is beyond intellect, beyond concepts, beyond creeds. It's an awareness that cannot easily be conveyed in words.

# Grandma

Just get so you can follow along with circumstances. . . . When the time comes to do so,
put on your clothes. If you want to walk, walk.
If you want to sit, sit. But never for a moment
set your mind on seeking Buddhahood.

ZEN MASTER RINZAI

As soon as I got home from the retreat, I stopped to visit my grandmother. At ninety she still lived alone in a cottage next to my house. Despite failing health, she was determined to stay out of a nursing home and wouldn't hear of moving in with me.

Our relationship wasn't easy—we weren't able to communicate well. She never understood why or how a girl could have the strange interests I had. We had a lot of trouble being patient with each other, but she had raised me under very difficult circumstances. Even if it wasn't always exactly what a teenage girl needed, she'd given the best she knew how. A lot of my independent nature came from her. I was trying to give something back to her, but it wasn't easy.

Fighting over the least perceived affront to her independence had always been Grandma's pride, but with increasing ill health her old strategies worked less and less well. Unfortunately, after so many years, she didn't know any other way to live.

With Grandma I was always spinning around mentally, endlessly failing because I disliked so much of what was required, so much listening to her diatribes against everything and everybody. Grandma was the unfailing rod against which I measured how well I had managed to incorporate Buddhist moral principles into my life, making them reality instead of theory. However, when dealing with Grandma, I inevitably came up short, wasn't quite able to apply all those lovely ideas about how to live a clear life.

In Zen meditation, we try to still the incessant judgmental chatter we carry in our heads. I knew my judgmental approach to Grandma was making our relationship harder, but I couldn't seem to get past it.

I knocked and went in. She was sitting in front of the TV in a big brown recliner.

"Hi, Grandma, I'm home. How are you doing this evening?"

Her eyes were intensely blue, a sure sign she was angry. "Oh, good enough, I reckin," she said in a harsh voice. "I been having them pains in my eyes again, and my stomach don't want to keep nothin' down. They ain't anything on TV and I get so lonely here, but you're too busy and always gone and I'm just an old woman. You been gone all weekend, I don't know why you bothered to come now!" She rubbed her forehead with a bony hand that shook. I could feel myself tensing up. This wasn't going to be easy.

My ten-year-old son, Sky, came in behind me, tracking a little dirt on the carpet. "Hi, Grandma."

"Now look at that mess," she cried. "Don't you ever think? What'sa matter, a big boy like you?" He froze in his tracks.

"Clean it up, Sky," I said. "And take those muddy shoes off."

"He don't think, he don't want to think! And you're not much better," she snapped. Sky sat down and started snatching angrily at his already half-untied shoelaces. He too was mad at me for having been gone.

"Grandma, don't yell at Sky if you're really mad at me."

"Well I am mad and I'll yell! He's a child and don't know no better, but you do."

"Well, here I am, start yelling!" I shouted. She laughed and the tension broke. "Oh, hell, you'll never change, sit down for a while, don't run off so quick."

Her laughter caught me by surprise. Suddenly it became clear that if I could only be a little more open and speak more freely instead of withdrawing into silence as I often did, maybe we'd get along better. Whenever I got into a situation I disliked, I avoided speaking to hide my anger, but apparently that only made it worse. I'd always assumed the difficulty came from her, yet in that moment of laughter I suddenly realized that I was contributing to it as well.

"Sky, run over to the house and get the plate in the refrigerator for Grandma. It's macaroni and greens," I added, turning back to her. Sky grabbed his shoes. "Okay, back in a minute," he said, glad to escape.

I sat down.

"Grandma, I know you've been alone a lot lately, but I'm here now. I'm not going anywhere else for a long time. How's it going?"

"Oh, I know, you need to live your life too. I'm sorry I blew up. You can't help it that I'm old. Go get me that album in the bedroom," she said, "the big one with the brown cover."

When I returned, she flipped through the album to some pictures of me when I was eight. "Look at that, I been meaning to show you," she said. "Cypress looks exactly like you did at the same age."

"He does—it's amazing," I said. She nodded but didn't smile.

In her gruff way, she'd just surprised me with a gift of great value, a deeper sense of relatedness to my younger son. Of all the people in the world, only she could have noticed and given that gift. And it came in the same offhand manner that most other Zen teachers used.

Sky came back with the food, put it in the microwave, and sat down in front of the TV. He still didn't have anything to say. Suddenly it was clear why Zen was traditionally a practice for monastics who don't have families.

"Do you think you can eat a little of this, Grandma?" I asked.

"I don't know, maybe. Put it on the table. I'll try it after a while."

"Okay, I've got to get home and fix supper," I said. "Sky, do you want to stay awhile or come home?"

"I'll stay awhile," he said. In return for the company, Grandma would let him watch TV far longer at a stretch than I would.

"Okay, I'll check in later. Bye."

I left with the relief I always felt to be out of there. If I could feel more love for Grandma, it would be possible to do a better job, but I couldn't quite manage it. After trying for years, the only thing I had learned was that you can't make love be there just because it ought to be. My aversion to the situation seemed like Mount Everest.

In the entrenched complexities of family relationships, like the one between Grandma and me, it can be incredibly difficult to overcome mental habits. The more I tried and failed to be present for Grandma, the more she grated on my nerves. The more exhausting the relationship became, the more I couldn't seem to stop the cycle of responding to her anger with my own.

We make formal Zen whenever we come together and practice in a ritualized way, but we make daily life Zen in each moment by how we keep our minds. Either in a retreat or in a difficult personal situation, our minds are constantly reacting to what happens. From judgment and comparison come likes and dislikes. We seek and desire or we avoid and resist. Finally we suffer if we don't get what we want or if we get our desire and but then lose it.

This cycle of emotional ups and downs is mentally exhausting. Negative emotions are obviously unpleasant. If you're angry, nothing is right, everything becomes sour. But aversion and anger can be very useful. If we pay attention to these emotions instead of just being swept along by them, they will become a spotlight that reveals exactly what we're most attached to and what are our biggest hindrances to being truly free. In a retreat we can't avoid these emotions; we have to pay attention to them. We must observe how our minds contribute to our problems with endless self-justifying speeches. Anger and frustration are easier to identify during a focused retreat than they are in daily life.

When anger arises, don't suppress or stifle it because it's not "spiritual" or "enlightened." The displaced anger will just erupt somewhere else and cause more pain. Instead, observe it, penetrate it, understand it—it'll be a strong teacher. My anger at Grandma was a symptom of how I resented being pushed too hard with the demands of work, small children, and taking care of her as well. If I could recognize that, it might be possible for the anger directed toward her to dissolve. Then it might be possible to replace that anger with a more compassionate approach.

A few minutes later, chopping mushrooms at home, I was still back in the cottage mentally. Suddenly a sense of the end of life and being old and infirm arose. When I stood up at the end of a meditation period during a retreat, the backache that often developed would go away, but suppose I was ninety and the backache was a part of daily life. There'd be no escaping from the pain. How do you live with a pain that won't go away? Was this what it was like for Grandma? No wonder she was so crabby so often.

That night, after struggling with piles of backed-up work on my desk, I was beat. It felt so great simply to lie down and relax, knowing I didn't have to get up at 4:30 the next morning. And just as I did lie down, the phone rang.

It was Grandma, wanting something from the store. Her leg was swollen, and I'd have to take her to the doctor the next day. Stumbling out the door, I realized one reason why formal Zen uses sleep deprivation. No retreat practice makes the demands on time and energy that real life can. When those demands are made, we can't meet them freely and easily if we can't control the need for sleep. There isn't always time for beauty rest.

The next day I picked Grandma up and we walked slowly to the car. She braced herself on her walker, turning to get in as I held on to the car door so it wouldn't swing back. She pivoted around slowly and sank into the car seat.

"Now wait," she said. "I got to get these legs in. The left one'll go, but I can't hardly pick up this other." She'd broken a hip several years before, and the artificial joint was stiff. As she got frailer, moving her leg became harder and harder. Lifting and swinging it was becoming impossible. I picked up her foot and carefully lifted it into the car.

"Okay, let me shove over." She got settled, and I closed the door and put the walker in the back of the station wagon. Driving into town with her, I realized that there are really four parts to any human job: to take care of the earth, to take care of social relationships, to take care of the needs of those right in front of us, and to take care of ourselves. So that morning I just switched from number one at the aquarium to number three. That was okay, it was all the same basic job.

But all the way to town, Grandma complained about the doctor, who didn't know anything; the neighbor's dog that barked too much; the weather that was too cold; the way my children dressed; and how my husband, Jack, was always in a hurry. Her complaining about him lasted for at least ten miles. His worst offense, I thought wearily, was that he didn't drink or chase other women. She had no real ammunition to fire at him, and she couldn't stand having to make do with trivial charges. He confounded her long-held belief that all men were bums.

By the time we got to town I was angry too, tired of the stream of hostility. We pulled into the parking lot at the doctor's office, and there was a young man carrying a screaming baby into the next office. Furious and frustrated, he clearly hated the situation and wished he was anywhere else. It was easy to see the steam coming out of his ears—it looked just like the steam coming out of mine.

As I helped Grandma get steady on her walker, she snapped, "You wish I'd hurry up and die, don't you? Well, don't count on it, I'm a tough old hen."

"Oh, Grandma, don't be silly," I said firmly. But she'd noticed my increasing coldness. Self-control was no substitute for real compassion.

If love and compassion are what make humans different, like the Zen master had said the other day, then maybe this situation was some sort of cosmic Zen lesson. But at that moment I had more compassion for a salt marsh than I did for Grandma, I thought glumly. You can't be fully present for someone without compassion. You can't fake it. The other person will always see through you if you try to pretend. If someone's hungry, it's easy to give some food, as one Zen story taught. However, despite Grandma's great hunger, I didn't seem to have any food to give. All I managed to do, over and over, was demonstrate that there was no food forthcoming.

Zen training involves learning to perceive situations without passing judgment and then responding peacefully to whatever arises. Eventually, it's possible to attain a balance that is independent of external circumstances. This balance is not passivity. We still act to address problems that arise, but we can do it peacefully, freed from an emotional roller coaster. Without the emotional energy drain, we have more energy, and are more effective in the actions we take. With this poise, a sense of connectedness arises, and out of that comes the ability to live with grace, almost with effortlessness. This was precisely what was lacking in my efforts to help Grandma. If I could ever do it, maybe I'd be able to help her. It was a long ride home.

That night, Grandma's light was still on at two A.M., so I went to check on her. The TV was blaring, and she didn't hear my knock. I opened the unlocked door and walked in. Hunched in her recliner, her coat and hat on, she had her aluminum walker on top of her chest, grasping it so tightly her knuckles were white.

"Grandma, what's going on?"

She looked up at me, her eyes huge and frightened.

"What?"

I turned the TV off. "What's wrong?"

"Where am I?" she asked urgently. This was serious.

"You're at home, Grandma. Why do you have your coat on? Don't you want to put down the walker?"

"Where's Valdosta, are we there yet?"

Valdosta was a city several hundred miles to the north.

"Valdosta? What are you talking about?"

"A man came and said we were going to Valdosta and to hold on tight. Then we flew here and landed in this pasture, but where's Valdosta?"

"You flew? In the chair?"

"Yes, damn it, can't you see. Who are you?"

"Okay, Grandma, hold on to the chair. Don't let go." I called 911.

By the time the ambulance arrived, she had dozed off. When the emergency crew came in, she woke up again but didn't remember anything about the flying chair or Valdosta. The eerie reality of a few minutes before was totally gone, and we were all back in the little house, getting ready to make a run to the hospital in Tallahassee.

At the emergency room, Grandma's vital signs were fine, she was totally rational, and there was nothing life threatening. So we waited hour after hour in the little examining room while the staff dealt with several accident victims who had come in right behind us.

As we waited, Grandma became angrier, complaining about the hospital, the staff, everything that came to mind. She didn't believe my wild tale about flying chairs and accused me of lying. As the hours passed, I couldn't comfort her. And the more hostility she vented, the more anger and hostility I felt toward her.

Anger usually arises out of pain, and Grandma's anger came from the fear she was feeling. If I could have felt that underlying pain more completely, if I could really have practiced Zen in that moment, my own anger might have dissolved and been replaced with compassion. Doing Zen practice in that moment would have involved seeing clearly enough so that my anger didn't destroy compassion for Grandma or awareness of the connection between us. Even more, it would have required patience and courage to receive her repeated blows without striking back and without losing sight of her suffering. It would have meant staying personally peaceful and handling my own negative emotions as they arose without dumping them on others. And it would have meant doing all this for as long as was necessary. Exhausted and angry myself, I couldn't manage any of these things.

Despite all the time spent at the Zen retreat, the fortress of my individual self and its treasury of personal desires were still sharply defined and very well guarded. And the no trespassing signs had been transgressed. I didn't want to be up all night in a hospital; I didn't want to deal with the whole situation. Theoretical compassion in a book was a lovely ideal—this was just grim. But I had to deal with this situation, there was no one else to do it. The only thing to do was to ask, What is this anger? What is really being asked of me? Why can't I meet this demand with compassion and generosity rather than anger? Why can't I give freely here? The answers weren't coming.

Once, I had met a world-famous Buddhist monk who at eighty-something years of age had lived through the near destruction of his society by war, had seen thousands of his fellow monks slaughtered, and was surely the only literal saint I had ever encountered. In a momentary encounter, his eyes had transmitted a pure and intense love that was unlike anything I had ever experienced. I knew for the first time that love could be as powerful a physical force as gravity. He could have helped Grandma, but he wasn't here to show me how to do it.

We ought to treasure whatever love we are given by others, I thought sadly, as I got her another blanket. However, more often than not, we reject love because it comes wrapped in prickly layers of demands, conditions, expectations of what we owe and must give in return. Often we can't or don't want to meet these expectations. The unconditional love for her that this situation demanded, the mind of that old monk, just wasn't there.

Before we can bring unconditional love into existence, we must first experience it. To experience it, we must be in a state of awareness and relatedness to what we are engaging. If we can let go of ourselves for just a moment, we might experience love. Having experienced it, we can then develop the ability to manifest it in each effort we make and in each moment we live.

The doctor finally came in. Grandma's leg was inflamed and infected as a result of poor circulation caused by a slowly weakening heart. She'd have to spend several days in the hospital to get the problems cleared up and minimize the danger of blood clots. Her mental confusion came from a salt imbalance in her blood, not a stroke. Medication would fix that. After she was settled into a room, the doctor came by and beckoned me into the hall.

"Mrs. Rudloe, I think we've got to consider a nursing home," he said emphatically. "This is the third time this has happened in six months. Each time we get the symptoms cleared up in the hospital, but she goes home and it starts all over again."

"I know. The medication schedule is too complex, and she forgets to take it. I try to help her, but I'm not able to be there all the time."

I was worn out and desperate for some relief, but I didn't think Grandma would ever agree to a nursing home. A profound drama was playing itself out. Grandma was experiencing the disintegration of a life winding down and she was unprepared. Her old tools of anger, fighting, and fierce independence were of no use, and she didn't know what else to do. My desire for an easier-on-me solution and my mental resistance to the existing situation were draining my energy. It was impossible to act compassionately toward her when I was preoccupied with the relief I wanted. If I gave up the desire for my preferred outcome—whatever would get me off the hook—then I could relax and really be there for her. That's what had been missing all along.

# The First Noble Truth

All buddhas' compassion and sympathy for
sentient beings are neither for their own sake
nor for others. It is just the nature of
buddha-dharma. . . . The inconceivable dharma
of all buddhas is not compassion alone, but
compassion is the basis of the various
teachings that appear universally.

ZEN MASTER DOGEN

In trying to help Grandma, I was face-to-face with the basic Buddhist teaching of the First Noble Truth—the inevitability of suffering that can't be fixed in human life. It is just the human reality to experience suffering of some sort. We can't avoid this experience any more than we can stop thinking.

A widely misunderstood teaching, the First Noble Truth is not about passive acceptance of suffering. It's about realizing the source of the suffering in our basic ignorance of our true nature and our endless desires (the Second Truth) and then relieving it (the Third and Fourth Truths).

How can we live with the people we must but convert the anger and mental disturbance they may create in us into compassion and equanimity? We can't be very helpful as long as difficult people like Grandma arouse anger in us instead of compassion. If someone in our life is suffering, causing suffering, or won't learn from the situation, and we've tried in every way to help and can't, then what? Don't argue, don't use words, quit trying to force the person to change. However, don't let him or her drag you down as will inevitably happen if you keep trying and failing to fix the situation. Keep your personal space and focus on that person's well-being. Stay as clear as possible moment to moment, and chant or pray for the person—doing so will help in a way that may not be immediately obvious. This is the time to practice equanimity instead of anger.

We can't relax enough ever to realize some ultimate Truth as long as we're caught up in unresolved personal issues. Monastics simplify their lives to minimize such entanglements, but the practice of laypeople is to work through them. No matter how hard we work to arrange things to suit us, there is always a hook. As soon as we achieve a desire, the next one immediately appears.

If we're unemployed and going broke, we can't get along with a boss or spouse or child, or we don't like our body, then we're unhappy. If we are financially comfortable, emotional pain—loneliness, vulnerability, fear, or inadequacy—will sooner or later arise. We suppress these fears, surround ourselves with pleasant things, and stay busy. We mentally resist and try to avoid whatever difficult people and situations appear.

Even when there's no concrete problem, there's mental suffering of the most subtle sort, in the vague feeling that something isn't complete. What's the point of life? I have everything, why am I not feeling better? And even if everything is perfect, there's the knowledge that life won't stay that way forever.

When we want something badly enough, we really do think and behave differently than we do if we are free from wanting something. If what we want seems within reach, we maneuver and scheme to reach the goal; if the thing desired seems out of reach, we may not plot and scheme but we're restless and unhappy because we don't have it.

Even if we seem to achieve all our desires, we will eventually lose them to old age, sickness, and death, both of our loved ones and our own inevitable demise. This fact may seem remote and irrelevant to daily life, but death can happen suddenly and unexpectedly. Old people often say that their lives seemed to pass in a flash and age and physical decay have caught them by surprise. Grandma often said she felt like a young woman trapped in an old, sick body.

If we don't address these matters, life always has a little edge that prevents us from having permanent peace of mind. If there's a problem, we think about it, analyze it, and try to fix it. We make what efforts can be reasonably made—if we need a job, we try to find a job. That's fine so far as it goes, but something always lingers that doesn't seem perfect.

Imagine a little blue heron walking along the water's edge looking for a fish. A human observer would see a beautiful natural scene, but for the bird it's a do-or-die situation with far less margin for error than any of us have. As far as we know, the bird simply does what it needs to do and catches a fish, but suppose it had a human mind in that same situation. The heron would probably walk along with an endless editorial commentary running through its head. It would either be pleased with how well it was doing relative to the other birds, or complaining to itself about all the struggles in life, and always having to hunt, hunt, hunt, with never a break and birds get so tired of always having to wade through the water, it ends in a self-pitying note. Just once why couldn't life be different but NOOOOOOOOO! it has to keep hunting this damned fish or starve and so on and on, blah, blah, blah.

At least that's the way humans might behave if it were us out there wading along the shore, and look how much harder that makes the whole affair. All the complaining in the world doesn't change the fact that the bird has to hunt the fish, and that we have to face our problems. Fortunately for the bird, it's not human.

When repetitive negative thought patterns appear and a standard emotional button is being pushed yet again, try saying to yourself, "Ah yes, there it is again," and letting that pattern go. See the feelings and thoughts that arise as an old, familiar demon. Study them instead of being carried away by the pattern and see what happens.

Life is guaranteed, sooner or later, to nail us with something we think we cannot bear but will not be able to avoid. If we could eliminate the problem, we would, but we can't. For Grandma, the issue was old age and ill health. For me, the issue was Grandma.

We can use all the unpleasant, unwanted stuff in life as a path to awakening compassion, wisdom, and well-being. Feeling scared, angry, and frustrated can be the gateway to finding wealth within. When we've met our match and can't fix it, then we've found the teacher that will force us to find the ultimate solution to suffering. The suffering we all experience is a vehicle for transforming self-focus, arrogance, and judgmental mind into humility. Humility leads to open awareness and finally to compassion for others and the ability to act on that compassion. But this relentless teacher can teach only if we are willing to experience the situation fully. Only when we turn and confront the problem can it be eliminated.

We can choose to live our lives tainted by the unnecessary subtle suffering that an unexamined life is so full of, or we can choose to live relieved of that burden. To get rid of the burden, though, we must begin with a careful, detailed investigation of what in our lives creates suffering, where, and how it arises.

The most insidious and hurtful delusions are the ones we knew were present in the past but thought were finished. Emotional wounds that linger below the surface drain energy and keep us from being whole and well. We may not even realize they are there. This situation is like an unmade bed—ignore it as long as you like, but the bed is still there, and a big mess. The only way to fix it is to dive in and do the hard work of making the bed. It may be painful to deal with emotional unmade beds, but when they are made up and healed, well-being becomes a possibility.

Zen Master Seung Sahn once commented, "If the world did not have suffering, life would be much less interesting—attain the correct function of suffering and then great joy is possible." If suffering is explored rather than resisted, if we learn to experience unavoidable suffering calmly and patiently, with equanimity, knowing it will arise and subside, arise and subside, we can begin to see how it works and eventually resolve it.

Resistance to life as it *still is* after we've done all we can do to make it better is the problem. Our confusion over what's fixable and what isn't and our trying to protect ourselves at all costs make the situation worse. In recognizing the truly unavoidable nature of suffering, and in giving ourselves permission to explore it rather than just fight with it, we instantly relieve ourselves of that second layer of suffering that comes from futile resistance. Then the burden is reduced to something vastly more tolerable. We can simply do what we must do calmly and peacefully, and life becomes easier.

We may get tired of our struggles, become tempted to appeal to the universe, and say, "Make it work, give me my desire," but that appeal misses the point. The art of living well is not to get our every desire. It's to be well and whole regardless of what arises.

Doing this isn't easy. The key is to quit being shocked each time the situation arises and bites us yet again. We can stop beating our heads against that stone wall of unchanging reality. Take the situation as it *is*, work with it creatively and compassionately. By not reacting obsessively every time a given situation reappears, we are free to enjoy the positive things that are also appearing and arising, even with the trouble still unresolved.

Situations that have the potential to create small bits of happiness appear and disappear all the time, sometimes flitting in and out of existence as quickly as a subatomic particle. When we are so preoccupied with our problems or so out of touch with a situation that we don't notice these little opportunities for well-being and happiness, there is no benefit. But if we start to notice the passing moments of daily life more carefully, then when a flicker of well-being appears, we can enjoy it. Doing this gives us the energy to keep working patiently with the difficult situation at hand.

As we notice these positive moments, we can see what they have in common. We learn what gives us a little energy and strength, and we can cultivate those sources. As with any delicate new growth, the more we cultivate such perception, the stronger it becomes.

There is a Zen parable about a man being chased by a tiger. He runs off the end of a cliff, and as he falls he grabs a bush. He is dangling there, hanging on with the tiger waiting above when another tiger appears down below. A little mouse starts to gnaw at the bush and will soon chew through it. What can he do in this moment of extremity? He notices a wild strawberry, reaches over with his free hand, picks and eats it. "Ah, what a delicious strawberry!" he thinks in his last moment.

If we can notice and savor the strawberries that are always present, that awareness gives us the energy to keep going deeper into a difficult situation. We may think that if we quit struggling to nail things down we will become passive automatons. However, if we regard the tough stuff as grist for the mill, fuel to wake up, then we can keep going no matter how hard it gets.

When we really do this, a miracle may appear—we may touch the core of God's love or cosmic energy or whatever you want to call it. Life reveals itself as spacious and free regardless of the external situations that arise. Even the most extreme moments become worth living. Unavoidable suffering can be the key that unlocks that gate.

To achieve that state of awareness, it is necessary to really live in the present moment, dealing with our problems only as they are moment to moment and not fearfully anticipating a worse future that only exists in the mind. To stay mentally in the present, we must develop the habit of noticing our mental states, watching how our minds function instead of being swept away by the editorializing. Only cease to cherish your opinions, as a famous ancient teacher once said. We can't cease to have them, we can cease to cherish them.

When all our efforts to make a problem go away have failed and we don't know what may come next, that mental state of real not knowing is a fire wall that can be used to focus our attention completely in the present. If our thoughts try to wander into the future, there's nothing there to play with except the solid, smooth face of unknowing. Our painful situations actually make achieving this trans formation more possible. It is only when life is so tough that coping with the present moment is overwhelming, and paying attention to anything else is impossible, that we can focus 100 percent. Everything before that point is just an interesting idea.

Doing this sort of practice requires knowing how to take care of ourselves in the midst of the trouble. How can we swim in the sea and not get too much water up our nose? Whenever possible, take some time to just sit, just bow, just chant. Doing so keeps water out of the nose because too much thinking and thinking and thinking, trying to extract a solution by force, is the route by which the water gets in. When we are totally caught up in our personal situation, the thinking mind starts its painful, destructive, self-centered obsessing. Such obsessing only reinforces identification with the small self and its suffering. Instead, repeat a short phrase to shut off the chatter while focusing on the concrete specifics of the situation at hand.

Lean into the situation and keep saying, "What is this? and how is it *right now?*" Realize that you are not separate from the situation, and know why you are doing what you are doing. And try to enjoy whatever strawberries may appear.

Becoming willing to feel the pain and acknowledge it in a personal, experiential way rather than as an intellectual idea develops a sort of fearlessness. It develops the ability to move calmly through whatever arises without panicking or exhausting oneself by endlessly trying to eliminate what can't be eliminated. All the painful issues of our lives are the means by which we can practice the art of living this way. We must do this work for ourselves. All any Zen teacher can do is confirm whatever insights might arise.

Facing death peacefully is the greatest spiritual challenge, both when it takes those we love and when we must face it ourselves. Yet we tend to live each day preoccupied with our personal agendas and deny the fact that we and those we love are going to die. We know it intellectually, but we don't really believe it will happen to us. It's just something that happens to others. But if we live this way, we may die never having discovered a meaning to having lived.

Many people lose all religious belief when they come up against suffering and death as personal reality rather than intellectual theorizing. Perhaps we would do better to look into the matter calmly instead of continuing our ultimately hopeless efforts to ignore it. Each of us has the ability to experience the truth of what we are beyond the round of individual births and deaths. Many who have looked deeper have transcended this fear of death entirely, no matter what their spiritual tradition.

One Friday afternoon a neighbor's son died of a single gunshot to the head, and it wasn't clear whether the shooting was suicide, murder, or an accident. Father and son worked together as carpenters and had just finished an end-of-the-day beer. The son had gone home with no other thought, so far as his dad knew, than to work on his truck. As we sat around the kitchen table of the father's tiny house that night, he talked in a dazed voice of the shock that came out of nowhere. One thing was very clear—death often appears without warning and always is absolute. There is no speaking to it, no changing it, no making sense of it—it is just *there*. Before the silent and utterly absolute face of this reality, there is only great unknowing. All the words of belief, philosophy, and speculation fade into silence.

If anything does survive death, there was not a hint of it at that kitchen table. If there is some other form of mind present—some nonmaterial reality—we are as unable to sense it directly as we are unable to sense radio waves or X rays. We have built technology to perceive these forms of energy, but there is yet no technology to perceive anything concerning nonmaterial mind.

A relatively few humans claim the ability to perceive something, but even if their claims are authentic, the ability is so rare that many don't believe it exists. They simply accept the silent emptiness as reality. Many more try hard to believe their religious teachings but have no firsthand experience to confirm what they are told; they find the words inadequate when death actually appears. Some intensive religious practices, such as Zen, purport to train us to perceive directly a reality that is beyond life and death. Either we must live and die with no real comprehension of death or we can use one of these intensive systems in the hope that someday it will be clear what is happening.

Making sense of evil is an equally huge challenge. *Evil* is a word we use to refer to suffering intentionally inflicted by humans, particularly when the victims are other humans. A serial sex killer is evil; an earthquake, even though it causes great suffering, isn't evil in the same sense. Although it's certainly easier to say "the devil made me do it," it's not necessary to invoke some God of Evil as the source of such things.

Human evil can almost always be traced in some way to the limitations of the human mind and heart, to greed, anger, or ignorance of the nature of life and death. Humans, like all species, are adapted to a specific ecological niche. We are omnivores and hunters. But we are also a social species. The ability to empathize is at the core of the basic human tendency to maintain communities and care for each other. For some that circle of care may be limited to themselves alone, and their selfish indifference creates endless problems for those around them. For others, their care may be limited only to their family or members of their own cultural group. And for still others, it may extend to all of humanity or even to all sentient beings. Whenever we identify someone as not part of the circle of those for whom we care, whenever we transform our pain into self-centered aggression, it is easy to exploit and to be indifferent to the suffering that we create.

Some of our most basic behaviors, like the tendency of young men to form aggressive bands to contest with other bands of young men and our tendency to be hostile to nongroup members, served us better when we lived in tiny communities struggling to survive in a harsh world. Then, as now, they caused suffering but they allowed more aggressive groups to survive better than less aggressive groups. These same behaviors still determine who prevails, but they are far less functional in the modern world with its huge populations, limited resources, and technological complexities. The suffering they create is magnified accordingly.

Add to this the simple reality that we have among us those who are dangerous because their minds are injured by mental illness, such as psychopaths who lack the ability to feel any empathy and behave solely as predators, and there is the source of most human evil. And, like all other biological species, we are subject to the natural processes of disease and death. Our fear of dissolution and our efforts to alleviate disease and death sometimes make these processes more prolonged and painful than they ever were naturally.

Our work as spiritual people is always to seek to identify the underlying greed, anger, and ignorance we encounter. Then act to minimize and offset the suffering. When people are impaired to the point of being dangerous, we must restrain them and protect anyone who might be victimized by them, including ourselves. However, we don't need to hate anybody. Where is God when somebody dies in a brutal or seemingly meaningless way? God is right there, receiving both the victim and the attacker in accordance with their situation.

# Family Practice

Zen does not consist in quietude; it does not

consist in bustle. It does not involve the

activities of the daily life; it does not involve

logical discrimination. Nevertheless, it is of first

importance not to investigate Zen while rejecting

quietude or bustle, the activities of daily life or

logical discrimination. If your eyes suddenly

open, then [Zen] is something which exists

inside your very own home.

ZEN MASTER CHINUL

Grandma finally accepted the fact that her situation was unmanageable and agreed to move to a nursing home five miles from home. She began to make a few friends and wasn't as lonely as she had been while living alone.

As I drove down the highway with my son Cypress on the way home from visiting her, the late afternoon was as sweet and rich as a rose in full bloom. The heat and glare of a few hours earlier had given way to gentle warmth, the slanting late afternoon sun brought every color to a glowing intensity that was tinged with gold. Green tree, red plastic roadside sign, all were equally beautiful—their very existence was proof of the magic that underlies this world. The towering summer clouds were ethereal castles floating above us, swirls of ivory and amethyst in a sky so blue that it shook. In the distance rain fell from a cloud in a purple streak.

"Look at the light and color and sky," I said. "The only thing that would make this moment more perfect would be a rainbow, but that's being greedy."

"Look," Cypress said quietly, pointing just behind my head.

I craned around, and there it was—a double rainbow. Abundance, when it appears, is an awesome thing.

We drove a few miles farther in silence, in and out of one of the intense local showers. As the sun reappeared, we came to the road just before home that dead-ends at the ocean. Like everybody else in the area, I drove out there almost every day.

You never knew what it had to share. Some days wading birds fed in the creeks. Once on a storm high tide a porpoise chased fish onto the marsh grass. Sometimes, sky, marsh, sea, and the tide coming in or out through the creeks were all there was to see. On another day four roseate spoonbills sat on a salt flat. One time two courting bald eagles danced and swooped on the wind. I slowed down and hit the turn signal.

"Why are we going to Fiddlers Point? I thought you were in a hurry to get home," Cypress said.

"Look at the sky, maybe there'll be another rainbow," I answered, not really believing it or even wanting anything more than we had. I just wanted to drive out there and couldn't resist the temptation to mess with his young mind a bit.

We turned, drove past the point where the wall of trees abruptly stopped and the vast sea of marsh grass began. I slowed down to about twenty miles per hour, and we drifted toward the open ocean at the end of the road.

"Aha, look," I announced triumphantly. In the creek to the left, the biggest mixed flock of American egrets, golden-footed snowy egrets, great blue herons, and wood storks I had ever seen was intent on a school of killifish. There must have been five hundred birds in that flock. As we slowly passed, some swirled up into the air while others held their intense hunters' focus on the life-giving water at their feet.

We had needed to drive to the marsh, and here was the reason— to see the birds. We went on to the end of the road and turned around, totally happy. And as we turned back, there it was—the second rainbow. It stretched across half the sky, the colors intensifying as we watched.

"Look, Mom, you were right." My son gazed at me with a slightly awed respect that children almost never have for parents and wouldn't *ever* confess to.

I was speechless. Was something going down here? This was beginning to feel a little weird.

"How 'bout that," I finally managed, as though I'd really pulled the rainbow off. "And we get to see the birds again too on the way back."

We drove back up the road in the glowing color and light, a little faster than before. As we passed the birds, the entire flock took wing, and in the rearview mirror they were framed in the rainbow.

"Oh, my God, look at that," I exclaimed, swerving off the road and hitting the brakes.

We jumped out and stared, now truly awestruck. Hundreds of brilliant white birds swirled above the green marsh, against the deep blue sky, completely encircled by a rainbow. They hung and circled and rose and fell, all in the rainbow. It seemed to last forever.

"Cypress, never, never forget this moment as long as you live. When everything is going wrong, just remember this," I said as the birds slowly settled back to the ground.

He just shook his head. We drove back to the highway, into town, and home, the rainbow still overhead. Sky was watching TV when we walked in the door.

"Mama, come sit down and watch this show, it's really funny," he said hopefully.

"Yah, come on," added Cypress, rainbow forgotten. "You never watch anything with us."

Pretty soon we were all in a heap with me on the bottom. The program on TV wasn't what I would have chosen, but that didn't really matter. There is the spiritual practice of silence and solitude. There is also the practice of engaging compassionately with others, and the practice of correct relationship, which I was trying to do in front of the TV. Both types of practice are aspects of reality, but they differ in their scale. The experience of reality that emerges from solitude, silence, and being in nature is the largest scale, which underlies all species, all of physical reality. Family interactions and engagement with others is the human reality that we, as a social species, instinctively do and that a mother is double hardwired to do with a child. They simply operate at different levels of detail. Neither is more or less important than the other.

I looked out the window, and there was a great blue heron standing motionless in the marsh in front of the house. In a spectacular glow of sunset light, its silhouette was totally there. It resonated reality in its perfect stillness; time and space were infinite within the curves of its body. I was held suspended with it; the couch, TV, and room were gone. The moment lasted until Sky spilled a glass of milk all over the table and I had to resume the role of offended mother. I gave him a hard time as the social contract demands, but it was just role playing.

Children can teach us an enormous amount about Zen practice, probably far more than any official teachers. Their main lesson is that while intellectual and professional accomplishments are rewarding, they aren't the way to happiness. Happiness is, after all, an emotional state, not an intellectual one. To be happy requires emotional satisfaction. Children teach this. Lovers do too, but dealing with another adult is so much more emotionally complicated. Children make the lesson clear.

As a means of Zen discipline, of moderating the demands of the ego, the routine activities of having and caring for babies and small children are perfect. Parenting is the ultimate Zen teacher. First comes pregnancy. The body swells, hormones and genes that have lain dormant for a lifetime switch on, and suddenly a biological event of incredible complexity plays itself out beyond any intellectual control. The self-aware mind, the ego, has nothing to do except watch and wonder. "Whose body is this? What am I anyway? Don't know!" The body that I always assumed was there to serve me was busy doing things for the unborn child, and "I" had better get out of the way. This was the first hint that my individual ego wasn't the center of life.

Then my son Sky was born. Holding him, I suddenly knew, unequivocally and absolutely that I really will die—he's here to replace me. When one generation wears out, the next one is in line. This was a major Zen lesson. In formal Zen, a teacher may say something a hundred times, but it is only a collection of words, an abstract idea. Then it's said again. But this time, for no obvious reason, the world opens up, and the same words shatter illusions at the deepest level.

That day, holding new life, I finally got it about death, my own death. And with that came the awareness that I was only one bead on a string of human lives that stretched unimaginably far into the past and would, I hoped, extend into the future as well. Did it really matter if I did or didn't get everything I wanted?

One evening I sat by the sea nursing the baby—something that required no intellectual activity except appreciation for the simplicity of the baby's food supply system. Several cormorants, birds that swim underwater to catch fish, flew over us headed for their evening roosts. They, the baby, and I were all complying with biological laws that have functioned unchanged for millions of years—the birds to rest during the darkness, and me to feed my young one. After all the years I'd spent studying biology, being a self-conscious observer apart from the object of my study, the sense of self faded away. I was simply a part of the planet's living skin.

When I was up to my ears in dirty diapers, when I had vomit all over me, when I was too tired to change my urine-wet clothes that would dry soon anyway, then protecting my ego, insisting that the world acknowledge my status became a joke, a fantasy. My everyday small self was revealed for the hollow illusion it was. Not only would this self die but, hell, it couldn't even protect itself from a baby.

Once when he was two, Sky was in a swimming pool. He had a set of flotation rings on his arms and couldn't sink. All he had to do was relax, but he didn't understand that. He was frightened and cried and struggled until I had to pull him out of the water. Pulling him out, I realized I was making the same mistake with my career problems and self-image—if I would just relax, I wouldn't sink. Everything in the universe was perfect just as it was, despite all the equally real difficulties.

Children from time to time give great happiness and well-being in a way that nothing else in life can do. However, as every parent knows, they also give a lot of painful moments and worry. We've somehow convinced ourselves that children are supposed only to be a source of joy, and when it's not so simple we are disappointed, frustrated, and angry. We think there is something wrong with our child or the situation, but really there isn't. It's completely normal.

Raising children helps us to mature, to get past being utterly self-centered. We are forced to realize that our lives are not the only important things. Kids teach us to put someone else ahead of our own desires. Our children may be the first things in a lifetime really to teach this lesson, and they do it so relentlessly that we are forced to learn whether we want to or not. More often than not, we don't want to but we have no choice.

In raising children, we experience unconditional love not as an idea but as a reality. Once we know what it is, the task of the rest of our lifetime is to extend that unconditional love beyond our children to an ever-widening circle of friends, enemies, strangers, all of humanity, all living beings, and all of the universe. When we physically experience unconditional, nonpossessive love for something or someone beyond ourselves, it is the single best thing we can do. This experience makes us whole and well, and completely happy in the deepest possible way.

Back in the living room, the milk was dripping on the floor.

"Go get a towel from the laundry and use it to wipe up the milk, Sky."

"But, Mama . . ."

"Now! Or do I have to count to three?"

Having made sure I was serious, he slowly headed for the bathroom to get the towel.

Later that evening a full moon glittered on black water out the same living room window. A night heron swooped in and landed on the moonlit shore. Against the blazing moonlight, all the blackness of the night coalesced into the grace of the bird, its wings curving into a fluid arc that seemed to stop time again as it landed. Then it darted to the side, out of the moonlight, dissolved back into the vastness of the night universe from which it had arisen.

"Hey, look at that!"

"What?" said Sky.

"A night heron—quick, turn off the TV and lights. Let's see if it's still there."

Miraculously, both boys complied instead of arguing. We turned off all the electrical barriers with which we had shut out the larger reality, went into the windowed porch, and sat in the dark with the panorama of black sea, silver light, and pines silhouetted against the moonlight. The bird was gone, but it didn't matter.

We sat there in the darkness and the light, listening to the Boston Pops on the radio—two little boys and one woman all at one with the music. By the time the orchestra belted out its rollicking "Stars and Stripes Forever" theme, we were singing, loving one another, lost in the black and silver beauty of the night, absolutely alive in a space that was outside time—the space the bird had brought. There was no need to remind myself to pay attention. In that moonlight, in that moment, Zen, the finger that points to the moon, was nonexistent.

A few months later the warm weather had dissolved into what passes for winter in Florida. Brothers and sisters, wives and husbands, children, single parents, friends of years standing, a crowd had gathered around the bonfire at a friend's house on a warm Christmas Eve night. Deep in the forest, shucking oysters and cracking stone crab claws, staring into the flames, tossing oyster shells into the fire to make them pop, we were a clan, an ancient tribe of human hunter-gatherers living before cars and television.

Later Jack, Sky, Cypress, and I walked through the deepest darkness, singing Christmas carols under the stars on the way home. We found the car, and the headlights burst into an oak thicket in front of us. The shiny green leaves blazed with a million candles of light. Dawn would come soon, the Christmas dawn, gray and silent over the forest and the nearby marsh and sea—a daybreak millions of years old.

In our house, daybreak burst in with little boys who had waited and waited and would wait no more. "Santa came! Get up! Get up!"

It was a riot of little boy urgency. We teased them heartlessly, pretending to be sleepy and staying in bed a few more minutes, but they would be denied no longer and dragged us into the living room, where the gifts awaited. Shrieks of joy—the toy given up on was there! Excitement poured in like a flood that no adult can ever know again. Then all the packages were open, their secrets revealed.

I looked at the heaps of trash—the wrapping paper and the endless plastic packaging designed to make each trinket look more attractive on the shelf than the competitors next to it. I could have been ecologically conscious and not bought it. But try explaining that to small children who had been looking forward to Christmas for months. Nevertheless, all the toys came at once, too fast, and in a few days they'd be no longer interesting. And then the children would want more. This was the downside of Christmas—too much, too fast for children to absorb and then quick recycling into trash. The pile of loot would make them happy for a moment, but the long-term result was only to create more desires and the inevitable frustrations that came with them.

Desire, said the Buddha, thousands of years ago, is a basic source of our human problems. Christmas, once a sacred celebration of religious mystery, has now become a materialistic glorification of desire and robust retail sales.

I could sympathize though. Like all children, I always needed (not wanted, needed!) more toys, more books, more entertainment, more candy, et cetera. Pushed to her limit, my grandmother would invariably declare, "Your wants are never satisfied!" and that was a sure sign I was out of luck. As an adult, I wasn't above using that same line on my own children, and they didn't like it any better than their mother did before them.

As an adult, the hunger was more subtle—more accomplishment, more recognition—but it was just as strong. The Buddha was absolutely right: desire is the source of so much of our suffering.

The kids were engrossed in a board game, and my husband, Jack, had gone back to bed. I started to clean up the clutter, feeling more and more down about the whole affair. As adults, we become a little more considerate of others, a little more discreet in expressing our wants, but not much. A lot of the difficulties we experience in our lives arise out of our endless unmet wants as well as our difficulty in distinguishing wants from needs: If only I had a better job/better mate/more money/better clothes/thinner body/fame/a house in the country/a travel budget, then I'd be happy."

We often assume that happiness consists of a large assortment of pleasant events, sensations, and possessions. This assumption fuels the enormous advertising industry and has pushed the planet to the brink of ecological disaster. But, ironically, this needy state of mind keeps us from happiness and prevents us from fully experiencing what we already have. If we could let go of that mind just a little, a lot of healing—both individually and socially—could happen. Material possessions, social relationships, personal accomplishments are necessary for healthy psychological functioning, but they aren't sufficient to produce happiness. Piling more and more on top of what is simply enough will never do the trick. And, worse yet, a grasping, hungry mind prevents us from perceiving and appreciating what is right under our nose. Being aware of this dynamic was all basic Zen, but knowing Zen and living it were still two different things.

"Pick up this mess, you guys," I ordered the kids. "We can't live buried in it all day."

"Just a minute, Mama, we're just starting this game, we'll clean up it later." I doubted that but didn't say anything else. It was Christmas, and there was no point in spoiling their morning.

How did I ever get into such a bad mood on Christmas anyway? I wondered. The last several months had been preoccupied with my desires and efforts to achieve professional goals and to deal with Grandma. There had been endless struggle and frustration, a lot of worry and unhappiness. The Buddha was right about the connection between desire and suffering.

The connection between my wanting, grasping frame of mind and the suffering that came from it had become crystal clear. I understood intellectually the value of being free from this kind of desire. I understood it, but somehow couldn't seem to attain it in day-to-day living. This situation felt like seeing the opposite shore but not knowing how to get across.

Learning to stay focused in the present, Zen style, was the only thing that helped. I could make my best effort to obtain a goal but, once all my options were exhausted, I could refocus my attention from what was desired to what was in fact present, using it as an object of careful attention. Instead of half-ignoring the present, as I so often did, I could savor it, and let it teach whatever it had to teach.

When we pursue our desires in a self-centered way, we are like a trout lunging at a lure. The trout exerts all its effort to seize the colorful and attractive lure, but a deadly steel hook is hidden within the apparently wonderful thing. The steel hook of attachment represents fear of loss if we get what we want. It also represents frustration and grief and anger if we miss getting what we want. Either way, there is no freedom, no peace. Fundamental freedom, happiness, and peace cannot be derived from any external conditions in our lives, or from anything that is given or withheld by somebody else. So what is the solution to this apparently lose-lose situation?

The key is to let go of seeking anything that must be offered by others. Only ask yourself, "How can I help?" If nothing appears, then go to a sacred place and practice still, focused alertness. This approach may not result in an instant or quick solution. It may take a long time, but it will eventually produce a transformation in outlook that will allow creative solutions to appear.

If my effort to get something succeeded, I could deal with the result when it happened. If the effort failed, I just needed to stay consciously focused on what was already present. Just live in the present, stay with what is in the moment rather than worry about some future moment.

This wasn't an especially original idea—it was more a variation on the old chestnut "Count your blessings." Pay attention to your blessings, maybe. But the idea was useful; it helped limit the suffering that my grasping mind caused. The only thing in life we won't ever lose is the ability to pay attention, to focus, to be aware.

"Mama, what are we going to do today?" Cypress broke into my reverie.

"Do today? You just got all this stuff, what more do you want?" I demanded. What more did I want? I wondered to myself.

"But I've played with my stuff and Sky won't share."

"Cypress, your wants are never satisfied. Here, sit down."

I tried to explain about how pointless wanting was, but the speech was absurd. He was a child and had the good sense to ignore the gloomy abstractions of middle age. It was 8:30 in the morning, and the rest of the day stretched before us like an afterthought. What could we do?

Jack gave up trying to sleep, and we all went to a nearby lake. The shore was a subdued brown and gray landscape of cypress forest and fog. Cypress, named for these trees, shoved his new scooter up and down the road. He was oblivious to the flock of turkey vultures sitting quietly in the treetops overhead, watching his manic seven-year-old energy.

It was the winter solstice season—the world was at low ebb, resting, waiting, slowly rebuilding energy for the next growing season. Once we were outdoors, my spirits revived—winter solstice was what I'd celebrate. This didn't have much to do with getting things, it was just another natural cycle. Pretty soon I felt fine again.

"Christmas—it's a forced commercial farce," Jack grumbled as we walked by the lake, "and I'm glad when it's over." In my family, he was the major Grinch, one of those people who every year endured rather than celebrated Christmas. He rarely gave a present and didn't like it much when he got one and felt obligated by it.

"But, Jack, Christmas is what we make it," I protested. "It lives in our own minds and hearts, and we bring it forth with our imagination. People like you, who complain about having to go to the mall and buy Christmas presents, see it as nothing more than hollow commercialism. You haven't bothered to create Christmas in your own heart."

"Look," he said, "when I feel like giving a present, then I will, but not because the calendar says I have to."

"But Christmas isn't about physical presents, really."

"They think it is," he said, nodding toward Sky and Cypress.

"Well, then," I said stoutly, as if my earlier doubts had never existed, "it's part of our job to help them see further than that as they get older.

"Look," I continued, "Christians celebrate Jesus' birthday, Buddhists celebrate Enlightenment Day, and Jews observe Hanukkah, all in December. We celebrate the ancient winter solstice, lighting lights against the darkness."

"Well, that's fine, if you're religious or you live in Norway, where it's dark," he replied. "But this is Florida; there's plenty of sunlight even in December—how much do you want, anyway?"

I thought a minute. "It's just that the real Christmas requires some peace and stillness. To experience it, we have to slow down, quiet our minds a little, and open our hearts. If we buy the presents early and then avoid the malls, turn off the TV and its endless commercials for a few days, it's no problem. Make room, and there it is—the real Christmas, as clear and strong as ever. It's easy to find after all," I concluded.

Jack shrugged. Maybe he'd noticed the gap between what I did and what I said. We kept walking in silence.

Later in the day, I went to the nursing home to visit Grandma. I had meant to take the boys with me, but they'd disappeared to compare their haul with the other kids'.

The entrance was guarded by two sets of double doors, first wood exterior doors, then, a few feet inside, a set of glass doors. Almost impossible to get through for the frail wheelchair-bound residents, the doors were there to keep incompetent residents from walking off, I assumed. But they also made it enormously difficult for anyone to go out on the porch in nice weather. Residents had to wait for a staff member to take them out, then bring them back in. It was often a very long wait.

Inside, the double-wide hospital corridors were long, bleak highways of fluorescent lights and tile floors. The cheery little prints that had been hung on the walls to soften the institutional effect didn't even come close. A few old ladies slowly walked the halls, pushing their wheelchairs for support. Some knew where they were and some didn't. Parked in front of her room, one thin old woman rolled her head from side to side with her tongue out. Recorded music played, barely audible against the cries and shouts.

I had thought that when Grandma moved here, the issue would be finished for me, but it wasn't. Instead the situation grew to encompass not only one elderly woman but all the poor, lost souls in the home.

Grandma didn't like the place, and I couldn't disagree with her. I'd offered to get her into another home, but she didn't want that either. They were all alike, she was convinced, and at least this one was close to home.

Like most of the residents, she was parked at the doorway to her room.

"Hi, Grandma, Merry Christmas! I brought you a present," I said with a cheerfulness that I hoped sounded real.

It was a bathrobe and a box of old-fashioned hard Christmas candy like we had always had when I was little.

"What do you mean, Merry Christmas? They ain't no Christmas here!" she said bitterly.

She took the present and slowly unwrapped it, trying as always not to tear the paper too much.

"It's pretty, dear, it really is." She smiled tiredly. "I didn't mean to snap, but this is a tough day in a tough place."

"Do you want to go for a drive?"

"Hell, yes, let's go!"

I checked her out at the nurses' station and struggled through the double doors. It was a series of complex maneuvers, swinging one door, catching it with my foot, pushing the chair through, letting the first door close, backing up the chair, opening the second, and repeating the process. It had to be done just right, pushing the chair with one hand and holding each door with the other.

"Hold on, Grandma."

"I'm holding, watch my feet."

The truck was pulled up in front of the doors. I rolled the chair to the curb.

"Set the brakes, Grandma."

She locked the wheels and I opened the door and lifted her into the cab.

We drove around for an hour, reminisced, ate some food, then went back. In a way, the outing wasn't much. Nothing we did could begin to touch the core of being sick, being unable to walk, having lost her home and control over her days. I couldn't solve any of those problems. I couldn't heal her grieving, couldn't turn back the clock.

Just being there, sharing the situation, reducing the aloneness was all I could do, but just that seemed to make a big difference. I couldn't work miracles, but I could keep trying to help. The visits seemed like nothing special, like nothing much was happening each time. They seemed futile, yet something was finally happening, something important.

For Grandma there was the knowledge that she wasn't forgotten, and a brief diversion in the long day. In facing the enormity of suffering in that place, I began finally to experience patience and compassion, learned that they were more than words or ideas. When I was forced to slow down, to match my pace with that of someone who moved slowly, I began to pay attention to subtle nuances and see the details that were otherwise lost in the rush. It was a case of feeling the situation, feeling the need, then doing *something*. The knack of figuring out what that something was, moment to moment, took a lot of practice.

Like most of the rest of Zen practice, absorbing these things, making them part of life rather than just ideas, was an imperceptibly slow process, akin to the eroding of a rock by water or even the movement of continents over the earth. It was so slow that I really didn't notice any change from one visit to the next. So, as with sitting Zen retreats, it was necessary to do this practice over and over and over again. Finally, the day was sacred.

# Hard Practice

Students who would like to study the Way must
not wish for easy practice. If you seek easy
practice, you will for certain never reach the
ground of truth or dig down to the place of
treasure. Even teachers of old who had great
capacity said that practice is difficult.

ZEN MASTER DOGEN

The Providence Zen Center, a huge, rambling building covered with New England gray shingles, sat on a slight rise overlooking an open meadow in Cumberland, Rhode Island. Behind the main building and across the pond, the monastery was perched on a hillside studded with granite outcrops beneath the trees.

A cold front had passed, and the rain-washed air was crisp and clear. The light was so precise and glittering that it made everything it touched seem 100 percent present. Every leaf of every tree sparkled as brightly as did the sunlight glittering on the pond. The slender trunks of young hardwood trees in the forest around the monastery stood like pillars in the sea of rustling, flashing leaves. Even a big black ant running across the deck shone with the bright light; every hair on its body was crisp.

Massive wooden beams held the huge blue-tiled roof of the monastery above the light brown stucco walls. Sunlight poured through glass doors into the meditation hall and gleamed on the golden oak floor, white walls, and dark wooden beams. The high, open, raftered ceiling gave the room a spacious quality. The massive, elaborately carved altar with its brightly colored fruit and flowers, gold Buddha statue, silver candle and incense holders was a glittering gem. Ranks of sky blue meditation cushions awaited the forty or so people who would be sitting in a few hours. A solitary voice chanting and the rhythmic tock-tock-tock of a wooden moktak sounded from across the pond, where somebody was doing a solo retreat in an isolated cabin.

This was my first visit to a major Zen center. The upcoming retreat would last for several weeks. I was a knot of hopeful anticipation and nervous dread over the challenges that lay ahead.

After supper, all of us who were embarking on the mental adventure of this long retreat gathered in the meditation room. We shared tea, the teacher gave an introductory talk, and then we sat on our cushions for a little while, settling into the silent world we would share.

The next morning the monk who would signal the beginning and end of the sitting periods sat on his cushion, motionless as the morning sky. One by one the other people silently filed into the room. It was time to begin in earnest.

Stars glittered in the predawn air through the branches of a huge old tree. As we sat, the stars slowly faded and the earliest dawn birds sang gloriously, all but one, who was squawking! It squawked along vigorously, thinking itself as melodious as all the others. Or did it? More likely the bird didn't compare itself with others or envy them, it just squawked 100 percent.

For the first time, there was no agenda for this retreat. The goal was just to sit—to be still inside and out and see if I could maintain it over a retreat schedule. In several years of retreats, I'd never done it, but maybe this time would be different.

As in any other retreat in this school, each day began with one hundred and eight full bows—from a standing position to hands and knees with forehead to the ground and then back up again. It wasn't an act of worship; we weren't bowing to the Buddha. We weren't exactly bowing to anything, we were just bowing. It was a physical meditation, another technique to get the mind still and receptive to whatever insight might arise. It was a concrete way of letting go of egotistical certainty. Like any intense physical effort, bows stopped the mind's chattering and brought full attention to the present moment.

For those of us who weren't used to doing it every day, bowing was a tough thing to get through and quickly became "just do it" practice—do this bow right now; don't worry about whether it's number thirty-two or number ninety-seven. Paying attention to the breath happened automatically as I became more and more breathless.

It was a sort of Zen calisthenics. There was no ignoring how fat and out of shape I was, and everyone could tell who had been doing bows daily and who had not from the level of panting it produced. It woke us up and got a good sweat going and was as beneficial as any other regular exercise. But what exactly did bowing have to do with spiritual practice? For a long time I didn't understand it at all. It wasn't for lack of trying. I'd been trying to do bows every day at home and didn't like it now any better than I did to begin with.

On most days at home, bows were a quick way to fit some formal practice into the schedule when there was no space for sitting or chanting—like fast-food spiritual practice. But doing them was still a chore, like housework, and my bowing tended to be pretty hit or miss.

At that retreat, bows finally began to come into focus for me. In keeping a commitment, even a small one, faithfully, we establish an inner sense of integrity. We learn to believe in ourselves and our own strength. That in turn gives us courage to accept the full responsibility for our life and for how we experience whatever develops. Then our honor, strength, and integrity no longer depend on what mood we happen to be in, and the down moods seem less frequent and strong.

Maybe this was a lesson of doing bows each day. Instead of making it a commitment to the teacher and an exercise in trusting the practice methods, I could make it a commitment to myself. Out of this practice could come the ability to control my own mind, with its endless opinions and dislike of the physical exertion of the bowing. As long as it was a commitment to somebody else, bowing had a forced quality but, once it became a personal commitment, it was easier to do. Noticing when bows were easy and when they were a struggle to finish, and continuing to do something for which I didn't have much affinity, I slowly began to realize that while likes and dislikes will never disappear, an important part of Zen practice is simply not to let either of these govern one's actions. I might not "like" bows, but that didn't need to be a hindrance to just doing them.

If we can learn to let go of likes and dislikes as the dictators of our actions, then we can apply this experience to other difficult aspects of life that we must engage, be they personal relationships, work situations, or health problems. Likes and dislikes never disappear, but they can lose their authoritarian power.

Some days the bows went smoothly. Occasionally they caused a sensation of effortless flowing, with conscious mind irrelevant to what was happening. If bows were like that all the time, they would be a daily reminder of how to live. On other days doing them wasn't smooth at all. Getting into the zone was one thing, staying there was another. At least this wasn't Tibetan Buddhism, where people start by doing one hundred thousand bows, which can take several years to complete. You've really done something when you finish that—and what do you get? You are told to do a hundred thousand of something else. There's no end to bows, there's no magic prize in spiritual practice, just the endless doing of it.

All week we sat and experienced each day passing—the sun moving from one side of the sky to the other and piercing dawn calls of birds in the suburban forest that blanketed the rolling New England ridges around the center. I tried to focus on the breath, watching my mind more aggressively than usual. A lot of the benefits of Zen practice can't occur until this basic skill of sustained focus is really mastered. I would try to make that my main effort during this retreat.

It was incredible how much of my mental activity was endlessly replaying conversations and statements I had made in the last few days. As soon as I forgot to focus on my breath, the broken record started again.

Getting up at 4:30 in the morning was fine for the first time ever. Sleepiness and exhaustion had ceased to be problems, and there was no caffeine craving or the splitting headache that often goes with a sudden total absence of caffeine.

During a predawn period of walking meditation, we left the building and walked in a long line outside. The moon was nearly full. Only a few of the brightest stars were visible that morning. None of those stars was saying, "I'm bright, I'm strong," they were just shining regardless of whether their image was visible or not. The stars taught what they had to teach by being themselves, with no self-awareness or wanting anything back. As we headed back to the building, the night's darkness found its last refuge in the black backside of a tree silhouetted against the bright dawn sky.

During the next sitting period, I tried to sit peacefully and calmly, and succeeded a good bit of time. Sometimes sleepiness came but not too often, and sometimes a backache but not too bad. Maybe sitting became easier because I quit wanting anything from it except the experience it gave. This state was the first stage of slowing down, and moving into the slow rhythms of nature—dawn, midday, dusk, sun, rain. If we do that long enough, peace and quiet seep into our hearts and minds. When that peace is present, so is the possibility of insight.

At the end of the sitting, we left the meditation hall in the dim, gray light of early morning. When we came back after breakfast for the late morning sitting, the room was full of sunlight, with the shadows of willow leaves playing on the floor—a gift with no giver. The rows of silent, gray-clad sitters blended perfectly into the airy, beautiful room. The uniform clothes not only removed distractions but also allowed us to become part of the overall aesthetic composition of the setting. We released some individuality in order to become part of a larger whole. Individual minds struggled to perceive the role of the individual within the whole reality. The formal beauty of the still line of seated figures against the white walls and sunlit glass doors, the sharp contrast of sunlight and shadow on faces, these were part of the heightened awareness of visual beauty and sound that always came during a retreat.

I really like this, I thought.

Then, something answered: "You fool! You went to Zen to learn how to avoid attachment and the suffering it causes, but now you're just getting attached to the method for avoiding attachment."

Another long retreat was not something that I could do anytime soon. Only when I was old and unattached would this be okay. There would be suffering in that too—loneliness, probably. Attachments and anticipations never stop arising. The point of Zen practice isn't to eliminate them but to allow us to recognize them before they have a chance to dig in and cause suffering. Enjoy the momentary thing but be free from needing it.

During a retreat, everything becomes intensified into a kaleido-scope of experience. The moments when we can't stay awake, the moments when the taste of honey or the sharpness of an apple are intensely present, the dance of energy in one moment and the mental blockage in another, these are the raw materials with which we work.

The morning sun streaked across the wooden deck that wrapped around the hall and shone on some trees on the hillside next to the building. A passing breeze shook their leaves. Morning sunlight and breeze in a forest—it was so lovely and clear. Yet most people in the morning leave the house, get in the car, sit in the office, and are totally removed from simply seeing sun and breeze in a forest.

There were individual interviews with the teacher that morning. The main purpose of these interviews was to work with koans, the famous verbal puzzles of the Zen tradition. These are questions that have no rational answers. What is the sound of one hand clapping? Can you show me your face before your parents were born? There are correct answers, but they will be attained only after all the rational answers, all the clever approaches are exhausted.

When I entered the room, bowed, and sat down, the teacher immediately said, "Zen Master Hyang Eom said, 'It is like a man up a tree who is hanging from a branch by his teeth—his hands cannot grasp a bough, his feet cannot touch the tree—he is tied and bound. Another man under the tree asks him, 'Why did Bodhidharma come to China?' [Bodhidharma was the Indian monk who came to China and founded the Zen tradition.] If he does not answer, he evades his duty and will be killed. If he answers, he loses his life. If you are in the tree, how can you stay alive?"

The Zen master leaned back, smiled, and waited to see what I had, but I had nothing, nada. After an endless minute or so, she laughed.

"That's don't know mind. Just keep that mind."

She posed another koan. I took a wild guess, and she shook her head. "You're scratching your right foot when your left foot itches!"

Another shot in the dark. This one yielded, "The dog runs after the bone." Whatever that meant, it clearly wasn't a compliment.

"Maybe it would be better if there were not so many koans coming at me at one time," I complained. She said, "No, do more!" and released a barrage of questions until my analytical, egotistical mind imploded and there really was only not knowing.

I sat there like a block of wood, and she laughed.

"The gift of the koan is the question. It creates 'don't know mind.' The koan you've answered is dead. The one you haven't answered has the potential to bring the mind to a focus that will cut through all ignorance. Koans aren't about keeping score—how many are answered, how many aren't. They're a dynamic dance of energy going back and forth between the teacher and the student. If you don't know the answer, just don't know! don't know! until out of that not knowing the answer will come."

Back in the meditation room, my mind kept spinning. You're hanging there. What can you do, what can you do? It was a stone wall of don't know mind. Koans are designed to produce that mental state in case daily life doesn't.

Koans teach in parables and provide simplified models of how to act with clarity in specific situations. They are also used to train the mind in making small intuitive leaps—one koan answer at a time—which in turn prepare the mind for the huge intuitive connection that is Enlightenment.

Being in a koan interview is a little like riding a rodeo horse. The student is the rider, trying to stay focused while meeting the verbal challenges posed by the teacher in a free, spontaneous, intuitive manner. The teacher is the horse, testing the rider's insight to his or her uttermost limits. The game isn't about never being thrown, it's about how long the rider will stay up. The difference between the rodeo and the interview is compassion. The horse only wants to get rid of the rider, only cares for itself. The Zen teacher, having thrown the student, picks him or her up, brushes off the dust, and tries to show the student how to stay up longer next time.

There are several ways to answer a koan. We may work through a lot of wrong answers, closing in slowly through a process of elimination, picking up a clue here and there from the teacher's comments. It's a fundamentally rational process, but one that requires some understanding of Zen practice. There's usually a lot of this systematic approach in the first koans we answer.

But if we focus on the situation in the koan until we are living it ourselves, then boom! The answer is there and obvious, and it's the only possible way we could respond. The answer appears out of nowhere, with no conscious thought or effort, with absolute confidence. We really begin to understand that there is a spontaneous, intuitive side to consciousness and that we can trust it to appear as we become more clear in our practice.

In either case, we struggle with the paradox and fail to resolve it until we finally reach a state of "just don't know," of stillness, the point before thinking. This is the launchpad for discovery, for new awareness of self and other, the core of the practice.

There are many koans with many answers, but in some way they all ask the same thing. They set up a given situation and then demand "Show me reality!" or "Show me how one behaves in this situation, knowing reality." The student answers by demonstrating reality in the situation described.

The answer is always simple and intrinsic to the story. But getting that answer is only a small part of koan practice. In answering koans, we begin to experience intuitive, nonlinear thinking. If there is underlying clarity and awareness, answers will arise spontaneously. For most of us, it takes years of rigorous practice to get to that point.

The answer must be consistent with the situation in the koan. An approach that works for one koan is summarily dismissed for another. There is no way that always works, so we have to be flexible. One may attain an intellectual understanding of the question and be able to answer the koan rationally, but the teacher never accepts such an answer. Rather the teacher waits for the spontaneously arising nonlogical answer that illustrates how the understanding can be applied to daily living in a concrete situation. A rational answer is merely abstract principle, while the "right answer" involves living and enacting the point of the solution, not just stating it.

As we work with koans, we learn a lot about ourselves, and how the ego protects itself. We want to answer the question posed so persistently by the teacher, and because of that desire to succeed, attachment, desire, and ego are in full bloom. When the answer comes, we learn something, we feel good, proud of ourselves a little, and the insidious ego gets fed. It's there again and again, demanding food when we least expect it, and we see it fully exposed through this process.

If we really get stuck on a koan, we will try every possible answer over months, or sometimes years, and they're all wrong and finally we find the one that has to be correct and it's wrong too. There's a lot to learn in this situation. Feeling the frustration, the anger, the aggravation that arise, we say to ourselves, What is this? Thought I was past all that, thought I was pretty clear already. Fooled again!

Unanswered koans keep us honest and make it impossible to

develop yet more egotism based on spiritual effort. Koans are there to keep us from coasting. They are a teaching technique that keeps retreat practice from becoming tedious. They convey teaching in a playful way and help us be a bit more humble and questioning.

The major difference between a seasoned Zen sitter and a beginner isn't in the ability to answer koans. Most koans can be answered given enough interviews. Settling for knowing a few koan answers misses the point. That is like a bird-watcher adding names to a life list without perceiving the birds themselves. The critical difference is the willingness to live the rigorous, spare life of a Zen retreat day after day after day, to sit still hour after hour and see what happens.

In the next interview, early the following morning, the hanging from a branch koan was still hopeless. After a few minutes the teacher started challenging the few correct answers I had for other koans. She was checking to see if I believed in myself enough to stay with those answers regardless of what an authority figure said. I did respond correctly but too slowly and hesitantly—she almost had me.

Traditional Zen practice comes from an authoritarian Asian system. Western students, particularly Americans, are often uncomfortable with this fact. Hierarchical systems of any sort have enormous potential for becoming oppressive. In order to function in a helpful way, such systems are dependent on the integrity and wisdom, compassion and energy of the individuals who are in authority. Such systems also require that those who accept that authority have a good understanding of why the systems are structured the way they are. If the people in authority are not clear and compassionate, problems and abuse will almost inevitably arise.

However, the hierarchical approach in Zen is full of mechanisms for challenging authority. The formality provides endless tests to determine when the student has become clear and strong enough to see through the hierarchy. The system is designed to empower the individual totally, but it does so through struggle and experience rather than by intellectual discussion in a group setting. One cannot progress in Zen training without cutting through the hierarchy, and challenging the authority figure in a clear and profound way that is based on one's personal insight.

Traditional koans are full of these challenges. They occur in dialogue with the teacher. Attempting to dismantle the formalism and techniques of the retreat itself is not necessary. In confronting formal authority, one can achieve an unshakable belief in one's self as well as a more profound understanding of the nature of that self.

The teacher constantly tests one's strength and confidence in order to gauge how best to help one's progress. He or she may start to deny every correct koan answer the student has. Such denial is a method for encouraging independence, and weaning the student from the need for the teacher's approval. When the student at last knows who he or she is and has solid confidence, it is possible to defy the teacher's efforts to create confusion. This is what the teacher is aiming for all along. Untested strength and confidence are never as sound as strength that has met a test successfully. The teacher's authority also keeps the student from settling for a superficial, comfortable answer to the fundamental questions of life when the teacher knows from personal experience that further effort will reveal an even more profound picture.

By the first day of the second week of the retreat, I was angry at the system because I was once again fighting drowsiness instead of just being able to enjoy the retreat. Once again, just getting up each morning was a test of commitment and strength.

All through the early morning sitting, I was preoccupied with how formal practice did and didn't fit in with family commitments, and I couldn't wake up. Mental energy, I suddenly realized, can control sleepiness. When there was less worry and more energy, sleepiness wasn't a problem. When energy failed, sleepiness appeared like a scavenger to pick my bones.

When I described the sleepiness at the next interview, the teacher pointed out that constant mental chatter and thinking require a lot of energy and make one tired. "There are several sources of sleepiness in meditation. Aside from the physical need for rest, sleepiness can be a subconscious way of avoiding the situation. When, not if, you get sleepy," she said, "try to observe it and note its sensations. Are there particular emotions associated with it? What's happening that you don't like? Keep your eyes open, do walking meditation. Deal with it awhile."

It made sense. As the mind calms down, one does feel less tired and need less sleep. A lot of the food we eat is to fuel the brain, so maybe a lot of the sleep we need is to rest it from its spinning. The world does look a little different with less sleep. The day-night day-night perception of how time passes may begin to change, and insight may develop a little more easily. It is possible to develop a clear, powerful mind that is no longer such a slave to physical demands. A sheltered and structured meditation retreat is a better place to practice this skill than in the midst of daily demands.

But the familiar schedule still seemed harder than usual—getting up, being tired, and doing all the sitting. It was definitely tougher in this long retreat, maybe because I didn't have anything better to think about. It was a good example of the kind of thinking that makes us even more tired, things like comparing this and that, liking this, not that.

My habit of trying to understand Zen and koans was partly the result of years of analytical scientific training. However, my habit of analysis also allowed me to avoid being intimate with my feelings. Intellectualizing and abstracting practice was a defense against living it. It was okay to "figure it out" as long as that was a secondary part of the practice, used to help people through their tough spots. But if I used "figuring it out" to insulate myself from the silent fire of practice, it would subvert the whole thing.

All this thinking! What had happened to the peaceful mind I'd had at the beginning? Now I was lying in bed figuring out the process of figuring things out when I needed to be asleep. It took so long to get to sleep that I was sure the next 4:30 A.M. wake-up would be horrible. I got up thinking, "The body will be tough. Don't add mental hassles. Just do it peacefully." And getting up wasn't too bad.

Once again, physical energy came from the state of my mind independent of sleep. The level of mental tension made sitting physically hard one day and easy the next. If I could stay in this retreat for several months, maybe I could explore that relationship enough to resolve it finally. But there wasn't that much time.

What would this day bring? I had a secret illegal stash of chocolate I'd been saving until it was needed. After almost no sleep the night before, this was the morning, and the candy was awesomely good. Out on the porch, the high wind that had been blowing almost all night long was gone. The stillness poured through me. This stillness was what was so impossible to reach in the meditation room with fatigue, backache, and guilt distracting me. Here was a whole sky full of awareness—a sky glowing with moonlight and early morning light, three stars gleaming through the branches of a maple tree and one dove cooing in the sharp cold.

At the interview with the teacher later that morning, I related the experience out on the porch and how frustrated I felt having to go back into the meditation room, with its backaches and struggles, to walk away from what this retreat was really about.

"Don't attach to good feelings or bad feelings; learn from both, accept both," she said. "When it's time to go to the meditation hall, just go to the meditation hall. And even if there's a special moment, when it passes, it just passes. You can't hold it, and if you try, you miss the next moment."

That night the Zen master gave a talk. "It's not so important to be right," she said, "to be a leader, to be compassionate, to be whatever idea you have of what you should be. It's just important to be *there*, and to be present fully. If you can be there, be clear, and trust yourself, you will know what to do with the specifics of the situation."

Several questions followed. How do you deal with those who take advantage of giving way to their needs? How do you handle an emotionally painful situation? Is it better to hide it or let the pain show? Her answers were basically the same. Just be fully present, be clear and trust yourself, and you will know what to do with the particulars of the situation. Zen never gives the answers. Specific questions are clarified but tossed back, teaching us to face and solve our problems for ourselves.

I began to relax and enjoy the experience of just sitting there listening to a talk. Everything was already complete for just a moment. What was I trying to achieve here? A set of Girl Scout badges? A little star to sew on my gray jacket for each koan solved?

At the next morning's work period, I was assigned to sweep some wooden stairs that weren't dirty. Coming from a household where hours were engulfed in a futile attempt to create order out of

never-ending domestic chaos, I was deeply offended at the pointless-
ness of it all. But by the time I got to the bottom of the "clean" stairs,
there was a pile of dirt that had been there and invisible. So! Pay
attention. Things weren't as they seemed if you looked close enough.
Unlike the endless, hopeless struggle at home, this activity polished
and repolished to maintain a high standard of order and cleanliness.
But using everything as a symbol of something else was analysis.
Maybe I should just quietly sweep the floor without all this worry
about whether or not it was necessary.

Although I was less sick with fatigue than I had been, I still dozed
at sittings, and meditation seemed about as unproductive as it had been
at any retreat. I was also having fantasies of being acknowledged as special somehow by the Zen master in front of all the others. Maybe next
time I'd come up with an answer to hanging from a branch so brilliant
and original that it would dazzle even her. This idea was more of the
endless effort of ego to reassert itself. It was what children do when
they compete for attention and feel deprived of it. The little child's endless desire to be noticed by Mother becomes the adult's desire to be
noticed by some other authority figure—God, the universe, whatever.

At the next interview, after my newest solution to hanging from
a branch died, I asked the teacher about my apparent lack of progress
in this retreat relative to insights gained in previous ones.

"It's not a linear process, and you can't measure what's happening by a simple yardstick like insights per hour. The things happening
are more subtle than that. The world is infinite, and if you try to
measure it by what you get and how fast you get it, you'll never perceive the infinite qualities of the world."

Oh. Of course. Whatever.

Feeling glum about everything, I went for a walk into gorgeous fields and woods with late afternoon sun that turned roadside ditch weeds into spectacularly beautiful stuff. Beauty was spread with such an extravagant, carefree hand on this earth. The sky, clearing after a rainstorm, was a spectacular white-purple-blue swirl. The natural things were such powerful teachers.

In the formal Zen setting, all the distractions of a social organization were a problem. Outdoors, human structure was irrelevant. If a Zen master teaches by pointing directly to reality, a tree, a prairie, a sea are even more direct in how they teach us. Reality manifests itself with no immediate awareness of anyone watching, more than any human Zen master could, and you're forced to let go of your personal issues when faced with that impersonal stillness—forced to ask only What is this?

Yet my buzzing human mind was as real as the straight stillness of a tree, so maybe if I just let the mind buzz awhile, and didn't worry about it, it would eventually settle. Even when nothing seemed to be happening at a retreat, something was stirring beneath the surface, because life was always different afterward. Things were always happening—the question was whether or not I'd paid enough attention to notice them.

Then came dinner preparation. I couldn't find some of the dishes that were needed, but unlike Florida weekend retreats, where a whispered "Where's the bowl?" was okay, no talking at all was permitted. Irritated, angry opinions arose in a flood even while somebody handed me the bowl.

It was an extremely simply meal—English muffin, peanut butter, apple, water—that really allowed appreciation of the smallest, simplest things. More opinions, this time approving ones, came but always with a judgment.

We ate following a complex formal ritual that involved putting certain foods in certain bowls in a certain order. Eating was done in silence, with one's attention totally on the food. Without keeping the mind totally present and focused only on the present situation, it was impossible to do the ritual correctly. The silent attention made things vivid and intense. There were not only the flavor and texture of the food but also the muscle movements and feel of teeth grinding into fruit. A saltine cracker was a feast. Not only a lovely ceremony and a meditation on eating, the meal was also incredibly efficient. The last step was to rinse the bowls with scalding hot tea. And then we drank the tea. This was followed by a final rinse with water. Instead of gallons of soapy water being dumped after doing dishes, only one bowl of clear, unpolluted water was left to pour out.

During the next morning work period, I was sweeping clean stairs again. Obviously this job wasn't based on my standards of what was meaningful, or what work was needed. But I wasted so much energy and generated so much discontent by worrying about the matter. It would have been a lot simpler to just to do the work to the Zen center's standard and stay mentally free by not being concerned with how my opinion differed from that of the staff. Sweeping clean stairs was used as a teaching technique, and it obviously worked quite well on that level.

Then I switched to a crew of several people loading next winter's firewood into a room beside the huge wood-burning furnace. Despite Zen admonitions not to classify the world into "good" or "bad," that work was a lot more satisfying than sweeping the stairs. It was essential work, something that a lot of human beings had done for thousands of years.

We were accidentally killing lots of moths and spiders that were hiding under the loose bark and got stored away with the wood. I pointed the situation out to the monk who was in charge of the work detail. "Yes, that's so" was all he said.

It was classic Zen. He confirmed the observation but didn't solve the conflict with the Buddhist precept about not killing anything. That was my job. We didn't mean to kill anything, so their deaths wouldn't impair our spiritual development—was that it? But this was still a selfish attitude. Tell that to the dying moth. Or was the lesson here just a realistic acknowledgment of the ubiquitousness of death and dying? If I wanted to take the extra time and energy to save those little creatures, I should have taught by example and got them off the logs as they came in, not just made speeches about the issue. Just get clear and then take action. But I also had to be clear about how much labor it took to heat this place, and whether we could afford the time to pick over every log with tweezers.

When the bell rang the next morning, my mat had somehow slid to one side, and I was sleeping directly on the concrete floor. That was fine, the floor felt soft and cozy. How else could I have known that cement could be so soft?

The next interview felt like an exam coming up—the Zen master was waiting for an answer to the koan. But that self-consciousness was only ego. Unlike an exam, there's no passing or failing in an interview, nothing to gain or lose. The teacher's job is only to see where you are mentally and then give you some help. So relax, I ordered myself, don't worry about making a good impression, and just communicate openly.

Zen is initially user-unfriendly. The silent meditation is difficult, the teaching is often illogical and confusing, and being put on the spot with an unanswered koan is uncomfortable and embarrassing. The living, immediate example of the Zen master, of someone who spontaneously displays the energy and compassion that Zen practice will produce, is essential to keep a beginner trying.

A formal teacher is someone who has more in-depth personal experience in this spiritual practice than students and is willing to share the fruits of that experience to help others find their own resolutions. A teacher conveys a set of techniques and practices that, if used properly, have been shown by centuries of experience to lead to spiritual growth and resolution.

Working with a spiritual teacher is like traveling to a new country with somebody who has already been there a few times and knows the way around a little better. A teacher guides us through the pitfalls of practice and can sometimes be helpful in the rough spots. A teacher's role is to hold up a mirror to the student's shell of delusion and ego. But the main job is the student's, to chip at that shell from the inside until it finally breaks open. If the student isn't working from the inside, the teacher can't do much from the outside.

Finding a balance between rational explanation and the paradoxical Zen teaching style is important. Too much explanation and the juice is squeezed out of practice. It becomes intellectual and dualistic. Not enough explanation and practice is too formidable and confusing.

A Zen teacher is evaluated by how he or she behaves more than by what he or she says. A teacher who can manifest well-being and energy in circumstances that would be overwhelming for most people will be noticed. A student might then ask for some guidance. Similarly, a teacher will evaluate a student's status by how the student behaves, and what energy he or she expresses moment to moment. If the student describes some past magic moment, that's fine, but the teacher looks to see whether the student has changed in some fundamental way as a result of it.

There is no way the teacher can really know what happened

except to look at the fruit it produced. A teacher evaluates a student not by what the student may say but by noting demeanor, energy, precision, and meticulous behavior. A teacher wants to see the student's clarity in how the student lives. If the transformation that Zen can induce, which is recognizable to an experienced observer, is present, then the teacher can say, yes, the insight was authentic.

The point of Zen practice is not to get Transmission, to be labeled a Zen master, although that can happen. The main goals are to become clear, to manifest reality, and to realize compassionate action in whatever circumstances arise. If one is focused on titles or on recognition of one's position in an organization, one has missed the point. One cannot become a master as long as becoming a master is a goal. It's one of the endless ironies and paradoxes of Zen practice.

A Zen teacher doesn't say, "Here's the way it is, take my word for it because I had some special experience." Teaching Zen means only pointing out the way that each student must privately walk. A teacher makes only limited attempts to explain Zen verbally and rationally. Instead the teacher gives the student techniques that can be employed to attain understanding directly, if the student uses them intensely enough.

Advice from a Zen teacher is important, but the role of a teacher's words is limited. They are only a catalyst. They may trigger something, but the actual insight comes from the student's own focused efforts. The teacher can't give the insight, or do the hard work. He or she can only provide a little guidance in how to proceed.

Transmission, being granted the formal status of Zen master, is not based solely on what someone has realized. It includes how willing that person is to compromise personal comforts to act on that realization. One can be compassionate at a safe distance, but trying to help in person is more of a challenge. Being a teacher means just being there for whoever comes in the door, giving time and energy in an effort to help those people deal with their situation.

There are different levels of formal Zen teaching. During a public talk, one explains principles and tells general stories to an audience. The more important teaching happens individually in a private interview, which is a lot more spontaneous and improvisational than a lecture. It is face-to-face, with the student setting the agenda. To be able to respond to whatever unexpected situation the other person brings up, to wade into the confusion and conflict that people create for themselves, and to do it in a compassionate, open-ended way requires great spontaneity and precision.

An interview may include some counseling, but an authentic Zen teacher should not tell you what to do with your situation, or attempt to control or exploit you. A teacher will only suggest how you can use your Zen practice to clarify your situation and resolve it. He or she will try to help you grow in your own insight. The ultimate teacher in Zen is the meditation cushion and the effort we make there.

In koan practice, the teacher tries to help the student see beyond the specifics of his or her individual situation and directly perceive the ultimate relationship of form and emptiness. A teacher should not attempt to teach such perception before having experienced that relationship personally and having had that experience tested and validated by his or her own teacher. Even though one may know some koan answers, trying to teach what they point to without a solid experience of Enlightenment is like the blind leading the blind. A koan interview is not just about teaching koan answers, it's about helping the student get to the point of directly experiencing the reality the koan only hints at.

Newcomers may tend to judge all of Zen by a single teacher. A teacher must be able to provide effective leadership as well as sound teaching. That person must be free to give the time required and take the inevitable setbacks in stride.

People who are attracted to Zen tend to be less than social, and the silent practice reinforces any tendency to be withdrawn. Nevertheless, a good teacher must also develop the skills to provide organizational leadership and the ability to mediate the personality conflicts and disagreements that develop in any group.

Can the teacher consistently be at practice week after week, even when only two or three people show up? A teacher must be able to do an equally good job on the nights when he or she doesn't feel like doing it as on other nights.

A successful teacher will provide a dynamic (more or less), clear (not always but most of the time), energetic example of what Zen practice can develop in somebody who really does it. The teacher will be judged constantly by demeanor, body language, and tone of voice far more than by any wonderful speech. If someone assumes a teaching or leadership role before having resolved personal issues, he or she will probably not be successful in inspiring others to practice.

Teaching Zen is simply giving. It means being there for whoever comes in the door. It's about giving time and energy in an effort to help others deal with their situations without expecting anything back. It's trying to help someone who beneath a calm exterior might be hurting in some way that may or may not ever be revealed. It's not appropriate to turn helping into some sort of private ego gratification.

Most of the people with whom the teacher makes an effort will come once or a few times and then won't be back, no matter how hard the teacher tries. Or they'll be very enthusiastic for months, then suddenly quit. If the teacher's energy depends on the number of students, sooner or later that dependence will be a problem.

The relationship of a student and a teacher is similar to that of a teenager and parents. The student must gradually move from seeing the teacher as the source of all knowledge to a more self-reliant, independent position, just as the child has to go through adolescence. As long as the student is still chasing after the teacher, insecurely seeking approval and praise, there is still much to do.

A realized student will approach a teacher as a full equal. Such a student will not want or need any help or approval from the teacher but just say, "Here I am, just like this. What can you do?" Then the student must withstand the examination and testing of his or her claim that will follow. When someone claims Enlightenment, the teacher will probe in some way to say, "Show me what you have right now."

There are several basic alternatives:

1.  The student did attain some insight and will reveal a mind of great love and compassion in a real-world, concrete way. The teacher can provisionally accept this and watch to see what the person does in the future. Is the person engaging in some sort of service?

2.  The student will get confused, back down, and ask for more direction. The teacher will then offer further teaching.

3.  The student will get angry and insulted at the lack of immediate acknowledgment and attack the teacher or the Zen tradition. Then the teacher will reject the claim and send the person back to his or her cushion.

After missing the koan yet again, I was full of questions. "Why is it so hard for people to perceive reality if it is indeed right under our noses, right here, right now?"

"It's not hard to perceive, but it's hard to believe that that's it because it's so simple. People can't accept that that's all there is to it," the Zen master responded.

Oh . . . okay.

"Why be so meticulous in our actions? Those stairs I keep sweeping aren't dirty."

"It's like polishing a sword. The more you polish the blade, the sharper it is and the better it works. Being meticulous is sharpening the sword of your awareness, of paying attention, it's seeing and hearing all the teachers that are constantly present, it's being aware of a correct situation, and knowing a human being's role and doing it."

Okay, so once more unto the steps with the broom, I thought ruefully. During work period, I swept the steps with a hand brush and got lots of dirt. Clearly, there was still a lot to learn about being meticulous.

The next day's work practice consisted of cutting brush that was in bud. I made a casual remark that it was sad to cut the limbs as they budded, and the man I was working with gave a long, unsolicited sermon about why it was okay. I disagreed with everything he said and was suddenly grateful for the silence of a retreat. Silence ensured that the teaching came either from within or from a teacher who spoke from years of practice. I didn't cheat by talking anymore.

That afternoon I gave up trying to focus on the floor during meditation and sat staring out the window at the forest. Once again some small sense of peace appeared. Hawks, wildflowers, a cardinal nesting, the New England weather flipping from hot to cold and back again—reality was surging loud and clear there in the woods.

I was still adding up lists of what I received for this effort. I still didn't totally trust that I'd be sustained without worrying about what I gave and what I got back for it. Maybe in a really long retreat all this incessant observing and speculating would just naturally fade away into stillness. Sitting in the woods and marshes at home was great, but it was impossible to meditate there for more than an hour or two before being swept back into the endless busywork of work and family life. Weeks or months of sustained effort were possible only in a formal retreat, where all the logistics were set. Then maybe some insight would be more likely.

An intense long-term effort couldn't happen until I could really relax within this retreat lifestyle, moment to moment, instead of counting the days until the effort ended. Only when it wasn't grueling and exhausting anymore, and the body wasn't utterly miserable, would I be able to focus. That might take a long time, so why not quit trying to rush things? I asked myself.

A day in this reality is not just another day aimlessly rolling by. Personal daily life is the froth and turmoil on the surface of the ocean. The bigger the waves, the deeper their turbulence reaches. However, there is always a zone beneath all the waves where the uproar gives way to peace. Find it, rest in the calm, and then come back into the turbulence and get to work.

The key is to view the sitting time as personal time that is the same as rest time. One can't do that until the aches and drowsiness aren't so overwhelming, and until it is possible to stay awake during the rest periods. Then they become the same thing, and the retreat is restful and healing instead of a huge struggle. Wanting to get something more out of Zen practice than the immediate experience of it is a bad Zen sickness. Just relax, slow down, enjoy the training, and then enjoy life. There's really no difference anyway.

Doing the retreat rituals or chores carefully is a technique to keep the mind focused, away from personal ego and its issues. Similarly with bowing, chanting, breathing, or wearing uniform clothing, we let go of the personal melodrama for a little while and become just human beings doing what humans have always done—asking, What's the point? All these activities help to keep the chattering, self-centered mind with its opinions, grief, and desires at bay for the duration of the retreat. Eventually that mind becomes less strong in all situations. When the experience becomes healing, one experiences a new perspective. It's not how many days until the retreat is over, but how many days of this special space are left in which to experience how life is when the mind is not continuously reacting to events?

The next morning I sat facing an east window at dawn. First a star sparkled through a tree branch, then the brightness and color of the dawn, and then the rising sun, glowing on the leaves of a tree, appeared. The gold, orange, and pink rays of sunlight in my squinting eyes and the iridescence of spider silk gleaming in the sun one minute and then invisible the next became the filaments of interconnectedness through which energy flows. Each of these beautiful events lasted only a few moments, then disappeared to be replaced with the next.

That moment, each moment, was an endless vastness of beauty, yet such moments arise and dissolve endlessly. One after the other, they disappear and new ones arise like water flowing through our fingers. There's nothing more transient than these beautiful moments, and yet there's an endless supply of them.

At a talk that day, the teacher began with an observation. "In this moment of sitting, we form a relationship with the cricket sound and everything else in the moment, with each other. The quality of our energy and attention determines this relationship, and that in turn literally determines what will happen tomorrow and next week. Sit steadfastly, not to get it done or to get a reward—just to be there, awake and alert, that's Zen," she said.

"We spend so much time trying to be something other than what we think we are. It's very difficult and very painful. It's important to just be in touch with what we are, to be aware of and enjoy the gifts we have, and to avoid the obviously destructive things in society. The way we are in each moment determines the quality of our life and our environment. If we really take care of ourselves, then we will also take care of everyone around us.

"When we are caught in thinking and wanting," she added, "then just focus on breathing to get free of it and get back into awareness of this present moment. Peace is absolutely beyond reach when there is desire, grasping, fear of the future, and frustration in the present."

Okay. Good advice. Sit like a mountain, and stay focused and present in each moment. I crossed my legs, folded my hands, and began. Half an hour later, the plan wasn't working out so well. I began to wonder what we'd have for lunch, and how much longer until the slap of the stick signaled the end of the sitting. But waiting for something to be over was throwing away all the moments between now and the end. Those moments are precisely all we have in life—why throw them away heedlessly?

The more we learn to pay attention closely, the more likely it is that any given moment will open into a transcendent experience. However, sitting in the hope of some specific result is wanting something. Being focused on desire mostly precludes anything from actually happening.

There had been easier moments than this in past meditation periods, moments of great peace and beauty. But even if I could describe one of those moments, it was of a past time. It wasn't right now, and right now is what is important, so what was happening right now?

Sleepiness was happening right now. It was the worst ever, and absolutely no flow of insights or mental special effects helped break it up. No matter how much meticulous attention I paid to being miserable, it didn't seem very likely to unfold into some dazzling moment of spiritual breakthrough. I'd trade the whole effort for an hour's nap. Maybe after that, life would be different.

It was really hard to pay attention to this moment when I was the next in line for an interview and anticipating that moment with the greatest aversion because I still didn't have an answer for the hanging from a branch koan. The koan was impossible and unyielding.

At the last interview before the end of the retreat, I walked into the room with a totally blank mind. Usually I entered armed with my newest and best response for the koan, the one that surely had to be the solution. But every answer I could dream up for the hanging from a branch koan had been rejected. Nothing was left to try. I'd just sit there in embarrassing silence until I was dismissed.

I bowed, the teacher bowed, and I sat down. At least it would be over with soon.

She got straight to the point. "Okay, Anne, you're hanging from the tree by your teeth, tied hand and foot. The man under the tree asks his question. *What can you do?*"

Her eyes bored into mine.

Seconds ticked by endlessly. The painful silence deepened.

"What can you do? Tell me!" she demanded again.

Suddenly something came to mind and I tried it.

"Correct!" She laughed.

Correct? *That* was it? My God, of course!

Walking back to the meditation room, a moment of mental clarity appeared, and I stopped. It didn't matter how I got to this moment in time and space or where I went from here. Everything was present and everything was perfect just then.

Instead of being still and experiencing it, and letting go of "I" in the process, "I" seized it. Ah, there's one, I thought. Instantly it vanished, passed downstream and away in the flow of the river of time with its floating debris of mental babble. Underlying the stillness of the Zen meditation hall, internal mental stillness and letting go of the ego is critical for this experience. There wasn't any, and I didn't.

Inevitably I spent the next sitting period trying to get that good feeling back. Was that Enlightenment? Whatever it was, the sensation hadn't lasted long enough to know. But striving and wanting to bring it back just made it more impossible. I was my usual semi-opaque, little, individual self who couldn't reclaim the feeling by reaching for it.

Just practice correctly and maybe that mental state would arise again sometime, I thought. Sitting in a meditation room prepares the mental substrate so altered mental states can arise unexpectedly. Maybe a master is someone who can maintain that state, express it, and act out of it freely and spontaneously, I thought, rather than having a brief taste and then wondering what it was and where it went.

Packing to leave, I wondered whether I was glad to go or would rather stay. Short retreats are good to clarify issues of daily life, but one isn't likely to get past individual issues and into the mental place where a more profound experience can arise. Short retreats are like mind baths. We do them regularly just like we take frequent baths for the body. The retreat washes the mind, lets it drop some of its accumulated ignorance, anger, worry, hopes, and desires. Then more time passes and painful mental states build up again, just as the body gets dirty again. So we go back for another bath.

Going between retreats and daily life may seem like jumping out of the frying pan into the fire, but which is the frying pan and which is the fire? We may learn not to make frying pan and not to make fire. Just moment to moment, do what is needed.

A dawn and sunrise couldn't happen in five minutes; it needed at least an hour. Maybe if I sat for a month, or a year or three years. . . . But that kind of wondering was pointless. Zen means coming peacefully when it's time to come, and going peacefully when it's time to go.

# Forest Zen

Know that in this way there are myriads of forms
and hundreds of grasses throughout the entire earth,
and yet each grass and each form itself is the entire
earth. The study of this is the beginning of practice.

When you are at this place, there is just one grass,
there is just one form; there is understanding of form
and no-understanding of form; there is understanding
of grass and no-understanding of grass. Since there
is nothing but just this moment, the time-being
is all the time there is.

ZEN MASTER DOGEN

$B$ack in Florida after the retreat, I headed to the woods as soon as I could get away. It had been difficult to stay in the human-centered Zen center and its heavily populated suburban neighborhood for such a long time. Beautiful though the place was, it was still very much a creation of human minds. I ached for the vast, open stillness that seemed so much more accessible in the forest and out on the sea.

We are the only species able to experience the full range of physical environments on earth, from seafloors to mountaintops, from forest to desert, and from high clouds to outer space. Beauty is spread over the earth with such a lavish hand that it seems to arise spontaneously out of everything. It's most abundant where the original landscape is still dominant, where we haven't quite replaced the intricate web of native plants and animals with the simplified human world of cropland and town, cut-over woods and highways. It is important to spend time in places where the ancient interconnections of nature still function, for it is the interconnectedness that generates the beauty and the answers we seek through spiritual practice. Whatever I was seeking, it seemed a lot closer to the surface when I was outdoors than when I was in a meditation hall with aching legs.

The gods of the earth always welcomed me back when I left the human world and resumed my training in their reality. In the wilderness, an abundance of teachers appeared, and they answered my incessant, fearful questions in the same nonverbal, direct-pointing style of human Zen teachers. At times, when I wasn't too preoccupied with my personal movie and paid attention to the elegant curve of a heron's wing, the air shimmered. Something profound could explode out of the smallest thing.

Tiny, crystalline ocean shrimp in their endless living and dying, orange butterflies fluttering over the barrier dunes in the intense blue of an October sky—their lessons are not about ego gratification. In the world of sea and forest, an individual ego is almost irrelevant. On the face of the planet, one human is so tiny; over the incomprehensible span of geological and evolutionary time, a single lifetime is so brief. The world beyond the pavement is a place to regain something vital, and to perceive the context of one's life. Every time I went to the wilderness, it was a reminder to relax. My concerns were not of such great urgency in this vast world.

Deep in a forest, I sat on a log to do some woods meditation— half meditation, half bird-watching. Gradually the land itself became more apparent, and the other face of the forest revealed itself. Things that remain unnoticed when one is walking and talking—wind, insect songs, and small birds—became dominant. The core of zazen, sitting meditation, was present there in the woods just as it was on a retreat. Distractions were a lot more immediate and attractive in the woods. After a while, the fundamentally false distinction between distraction and truth might dissolve.

The morning air was misty, and the rising sun sparkled in rainbow-colored flashes of dew. The ground was a brilliant green carpet of bracken fern that swept like a sea around the dark, straight trunks of the pines. The ferns formed their own foot-high canopy, like a forest of miniature trees with tiny trunks and spreading branches. Purple violets bloomed everywhere underneath them. I kept expecting to see a silver-white unicorn in the distance, or maybe some fairies under the ferns. Their absence was surely only because they come out by moonlight and it was already after sunrise. I'd just come too late and missed them.

Five or six deer passed silently among the trees in the far distance, visible only by the flash of their white tails. The forest was ringing with birdcalls. Gradually, the sound of the wind became the flow of time, the voice of reality moving like a river. The voice is always there and flowing, but it usually goes unnoticed beneath the clutter of daily commitments and schedules. Sometimes we clear away the clutter and notice it. When we sit outdoors in silence, we can make contact with a larger, underlying energy.

An old piece of pine branch lay in the grass. Winged termites were emerging and flying up into the morning light. Their elegant white, teardrop-shaped wings were twice as long as their bright little bodies. They fluttered up into the sunlight by the hundreds, until the morning air was alight with their wings. They flowed like a stream into an unknown world. There was no doubt, no fear, no self-conscious choice—just the flowing, and the entire universe was in that flight.

As I sat against the pine tree, with frogs, crickets, and the wind in full hullabaloo, a sudden awareness of continuity, and the self-arising organic nature of reality, arose. It was four-dimensional, extending through time as well as space. Tree and insect, foraging bird and the sitter on a log, and the bracket fungus on the log, we all were a piece of the same living fabric, just as were all the past lineages of primates in my ancestry and all the ancestors of the bracket fungus. For every relationship of which I was aware, there were at least a thousand more I hadn't seen.

Slowly, I headed toward a nearby lake. As I walked along a footpath around a cypress pond, a charmed space appeared. It was one of those special moments when the air shimmers and the magic of the world is laid out for inspection. Embedded in golden mist, the sun was just above the treetops. The rays caught water droplets on the grass from the night's rain so that a mesh of diamonds glittered across the meadow of wildflowers, wire grass, and palmetto.

The fall flowers were blooming—purple blazing stars, vivid red cardinal flowers, black-eyed Susans, and DYCs—damned yellow composites—the closely related little yellow daisies that drive botany students to distraction trying to sort them into species. This particular patch of woods was abloom with huge yellow false foxglove. Every fall the flowers spread their feast in the woods and coastal dunes as butterflies pour down from the North, running ahead of a winter they've never known, headed for mountain refuges in Mexico and the Caribbean.

And, sure enough, the butterflies were here again. They danced in the sunshine, swarmed over the flowers, and took on fuel for the rest of the long journey to a place their great-grandparents left last spring. Somehow they were going home to a place they'd never seen. Everywhere, yellow sulfur butterflies darted over the yellow trumpet-shaped flowers. The air danced with them until it seemed as if butterflies were flowers and flowers took wing as butterflies.

At the lakeshore, a freshwater marsh was emerald with grass, cypress trees, and arrowhead weed. Three great blue herons stood like statues along the opposite shore. An alligator sunned its back in the water a few feet away. Over the open lake, two or three ospreys were churping and fishing. The floating nuphar flowers were bright yellow balls against their green leaves and the blue water, but the motionless gator looked like something made of black rock—some lava that had flowed and cooled into a lizard shape. Suddenly a turtle's head, all black and wedge-shaped, popped up. The sunlight gleamed gold on the turtle and on the gator just beyond.

Neither animal seemed interested in the other, and the gator slowly drifted along the shore. All these beings shared this space and time in peace, except when they needed to eat. Why do humans feel so compelled to mess with what is, to exploit rather than coexist? I wondered.

The day warmed, and with the warmth came a rich smell of wet earth. I stood up and stretched after having sat still for an hour. The gator instantly disappeared below the surface without a ripple, while a black snake that had been sunning nearby raced frantically for cover. Then several flocks of white pelicans appeared over the western horizon like a smudge. They soared to the east in wavering single files and shallow V formations, their huge black-and-white wings flashing in the sun.

Ripples of vertical movement flowed through the lines of flying birds from front to back like an ocean wave rising and falling. In their effortless soaring, they were doing what they needed to do in that moment perfectly. There was no confusion or hesitation, struggle or doubt about it, unlike the way people struggle with their issues. That soaring was the Tao, the natural order of the universe, made visible and manifest. How did humans get so complicated?

Back at the coast, the carpet of sunlight was spread over the bay. It's a show that never fails. If there is sunlight and water, the dazzling display is simply there. Unlike human efforts to achieve something that may succeed or fail, the fundamentals of this universe are always in place. The light and water danced and danced. The answers to all the spiritual questions were right there. All I had to do was look. But it felt like staring at words on a page when you can't read the language in which they're written.

The tide poured into the bay, salt water coalescing into tiny new silver fish. The glittering sun outlined the crests of little waves blazing gold in the wind. Six or seven ring-billed gulls were clustered in three inches of water, next to the shore, alternately walking and floating as wavelets swept past them. They scratched the sand intently with both feet, bobbing their heads into the water every few seconds to pick up what they had kicked to the surface—clams, worms, amphipods, whatever. They looked like chickens or sparrows scratching in leaves except that they used both feet together, letting the water keep them up. Six cormorants sat as black silhouettes on black pilings against the gold-and-white sea. They were as motionless as stone carvings.

The breeze died, and flocks of little shorebirds raced down the shore and disappeared before I could even see what they were. Then they reappeared, bills darting into clumps of bright red seaweed on the beach, hunting the tiny crustaceans that live there. These birds lived in fast-forward while the ring-billed gulls methodically dug, and the entranced cormorants maintained their motionless blackness in a universe of light.

In the pinewoods behind the beach, three or four songbirds called loudly, dueting across the land. They stayed well hidden despite all the calling. A woodpecker started tapping, but it was invisible too. I had been sitting in the sun, but the long, slender shadow of a pine swung over and then behind me in fifteen minutes. In the shadow's movement, the turning of the planet was apparent. Finally, a bright yellow, little bird flashed against the blue sky and the green pine needles like a piece of the sun. It was a pine warbler, the source of the piercing calls.

Sitting there, meditation beads on one knee and binoculars on the other, I might never experience some transcendent mental state, but the birds were more present that ever before. Focused, disciplined mental concentration would have to happen in some spot where the birds were fewer —how could anyone ignore a bird?

And then they left, all except the cormorants dreaming in the sun. The sun, the sea, and the ocean of air above it, blue and gold, vast and ancient, was beyond human grasp. A bird foraging for a meal I could relate to, but the planetary scale of the ocean was beyond my understanding.

I turned to leave but suddenly noticed a mimosa tree in full bloom, and stared at it, transfixed. The pink flowers appeared on the tree when conditions were right. It wasn't the flowers' individualistic goal to do anything at all. This human life was a part of the same organic system—just like a flower on a tree, I was part of this self-directing universe no more or less than the mimosa flower, just a different manifestation.

This was the teaching of Zen Master Dogen come to life. This old plum tree is boundless. All at once its blossoms open and of itself the fruit is born. It forms spring; it forms winter. It arouses wind and wild rain. . . . It becomes grass and trees; it becomes pure fragrance. Its whirling, miraculous transformation has no limit. Furthermore, the treeness of the great earth, high sky, bright sun, and clear moon derives from the treeness of the old plum tree. They have always been entangled, vine with vine.

The next morning, I went back to the woods to chase that experience down again, seize and experience it a second time. But you can't make an appointment for that sort of thing, and no great insights appeared. There was sun and wind shaking the trees and a cacophony of tree frogs, crickets, and birds calling. Then something said in an incredulous tone, "You want more?"

# Conflict and
# Compassion

The ultimate principles that make up the Way
are not something to be thrashed out in con-
tentious debate, clanging and banging to beat
down the unbelievers. This thing handed down
from the buddhas and patriarchs has
no special meaning.

ZEN MASTER RINZAI

$S$harks, along with crocodiles, grizzly bears, and tigers, are members of an elite subset of big predators—those whom humans still fear. We easily cope with thousands of traffic fatalities each year. They are the results of our own technology, the price we pay for progress or something like that. But let one shark eat one swimmer and it's a media field day. Maybe it's the effrontery of a shark attack that we can't handle—the idea that an animal might occasionally regard a human as a mere meal.

Most of the eating is the other way around, though, and a commercial fishery had been developed based on sharks. A fishing magazine editor needed a story on the fishery in a hurry. A few days after his call, Jack and I were on a trawler out in the oil fields, the offshore city of drilling and production platforms off the Louisiana coast. Their lights shone all around us at night, and the monotonous blaring of horns warned us to stay clear. Here and there vents of burning natural gas flared. The huge hydraulic winches on the ninety-foot commercial trawler turned slowly, reeling in miles of steel longline cable. Every few feet a six-inch steel hook dangled from its leader wire, but most of the hooks were empty. Then an eight-foot blacktip shark came up, the hook solidly in its jaw. As the cable pulled the shark up to the deck, one fisherman grabbed the wire in his gloved hand and jerked the fish aboard. A second man slammed a machete into the shark's head, severing it with two blows as red blood poured across the white steel deck. Another blow removed the tail, and more blood pulsed out of a massive artery. The fishermen quickly sliced off the valuable fins and gutted the shark, and the lifeless "trunk" was tossed into the freezer. The whole process took less than five minutes, and the winch resumed its slow turning.

The longlines didn't catch just sharks. Equally predatory six-foot-long giant snake eels took the hooks as well. Most of them were nearly dead when they came up, killed by swallowing the hooks and by the rapid change in pressure from the four-hundred-foot-deep bottom to the surface. They were quickly chopped up by the fishermen for shark bait on the next set.

We watched the brutal, efficient killing of shark after shark, eel after eel. The blood poured across the deck, back into the sea, and the fishermen used every spare moment to sharpen their already razor-edged machetes. The sharks were big, sharp-toothed predators, taken in turn by the chief predators on this planet, humans. Their teeth, muscles, speed, and exquisite senses were no match for brains, steel, and diesel engines.

Mercy was neither asked nor given. In the sea, death simply means the transformation of one life-form into another. At one level this was okay. Humans are biological predators themselves, hunters with incisor teeth to tear meat. Somebody would eat these sharks. Perhaps life and death are not really so separate, only alternative states of the same natural phenomenon, endlessly moving eddies in a turbulent flow of energy and consciousness. But there was more to it than that.

Resolving the mystery of life and death is the great challenge of Zen practice. Inside the gate of the famous Japanese Zen monastery at Eiheiji, two inscriptions read, "Only those concerned with the question of life and death need enter here" and "Those not completely concerned with this question have no reason to enter this gate."

Being a predator is not limited to killing animals. We are predators in so many other ways. We are predators on the earth herself. We, like the sharks, are predators on our own kind, sometimes even on ourselves. However, humans have the intellectual potential to be more than just unaware, biological chief predators. No other species is known to have the ability to act out of compassion. And compassion, according to Zen, is the most basic part of the human reality. Watching the sharks and eels die, I wondered if we would ever learn to recognize and reduce the daily acts of predation we all commit, the ones that aren't as obvious as a machete cutting into living flesh.

After we finished the fishing story and went home, I was looking forward to a few hours of doing nothing more than reading the Sunday paper. I flipped through the sections and stopped cold. A color picture of a beachside condominium covered the front of the real estate section. It was one of the many developments that had mushroomed in the last few years on the ocean side of the long, narrow peninsula that separates St. Joc Bay in north Florida from the Gulf of Mexico. The once spectacular landscape of sand dunes, sea, and wind-twisted pines was slowly drowning in an ugly clutter of houses and condos.

The wealthy owner of one of the condo projects, according to the paper, was planning to build a huge marina in the middle of the sea grass beds. Sales of condominiums in the overbuilt area were slow. If the developer could offer prospective buyers a marina, he hoped he'd have an edge on his competitors. He also wanted a golf course built on land that was porous beach sand right next to the bay.

There was no way this could pass without a challenge. Polluted runoff from this type of development makes the clear, shallow water too murky for the sea grass to survive. Once the grass died, all the swarming fish, shrimp, and scallops that depended on it would be gone as well. A marina would require a lot of dredging to dig channels and a boat basin. The turbidity from the dredging would kill a lot more of the adjacent sea grass. Once the marina was in operation, the stagnant, silty bottom of the boat basin would become polluted with petroleum and heavy metals, and this contamination would spread to the surrounding waters. The runoff of pesticides and fertilizers from a golf course would poison whatever marine life was left after the dredging.

The project ought to have been turned down by the state and federal regulatory agencies that had to give permits for it. The marina alone would violate all sorts of state and federal guidelines on marina sites. But the review of permit applications was very political, and in recent years developers, regarded as "clients," were helped through the process. Permits were given, sometimes with a few conditions to mitigate the damage, but always given. Denial wasn't in the vocabulary if the applicant was rich and well connected.

This was a place where I'd done research and taken students for twenty years. It wasn't going to die if I could help it. I wasn't going to trust the system to do the right thing either, because it most assuredly wouldn't. This developer had a big investment at stake and lots of financial clout. Nearby Port St. Joe was primarily a paper mill town, its people not very likely to leap into an environmental fight. There was no local environmental group there. It was going to be me all by myself versus him, and he had millions of dollars.

I felt awful. From long experience as an environmental activist,

I knew how engulfing and exhausting these fights can be. Endless hours would be spent in hearings where everybody except me was paid to be present, as either a regulatory bureaucrat or a well-compensated consultant for the developer. The only reward for victory in most of these battles was the knowledge that some green and living place would stay that way for a little while longer. Maybe. Yet environmental battles are about one thing—understanding our relationship to the earth and trying to act out of love and compassion to protect and restore the planet. When a conflict arises, it is essential to wage the battle from this point of view rather than fight out of anger or fear of failure.

In Japan, Zen practice and the life of the warrior have a long, traditional relationship. The Zen-trained samurai seeks to be as clear as cut glass and just as dangerous. Today Zen is equally useful for social activists. Warriors and activists require the same basic traits—a lot of energy, the ability to make personal security a secondary goal, and the ability to sustain the effort through defeats as well as victories. These qualities often arise spontaneously as one attains some awareness, through meditation, of this living universe and one's position within it.

Anger and fear may produce energy for a while, but over the long term they only take the joy out of life, draining one's strength in the process. These negative emotions aren't needed anyway. Once a warrior learns to fight without anger, she or he will be stronger, more energetic, and therefore more effective.

Many of us tend to see the world in terms of competing opposites—good and bad, right and wrong. We choose our preferred side and find reasons to dismiss the opposing point of view. Environmental fights are cast in this light more often than not.

Zen, however, speaks of putting down our opinions and says that our ideas of right and wrong are just more opinions. With that attitude, how can we act in our daily lives, continue on in the reality that surrounds us? Are we to ignore the problems around us? Or callously dismiss them as karma, blaming the victims on some cosmic scale? Many Westerners, brought up on rigid ideas of right and wrong, good and evil, may assume that a system that refuses to sort things into good and evil is amoral. Nothing could be further from the truth.

Zen simply trusts in centuries of experience that cruel or selfish action is not very likely to arise as one becomes more conscious of one's relationship to everything else. Intentionally to cause another to suffer is to create suffering for oneself. Without a limited, grasping, selfish ego, compassion will direct our thoughts, our words, and our deeds. Thus our actions will be authentically moral and effective. An external set of rules and punishments is simply extraneous and unnecessary. We can engage all of life—including the painful, unsavory, and even appalling aspects, as well as the more acceptable parts—with equanimity. When self-centered desire produces other forms of behavior, the Zen practice of routine self-examination will expose the weakness for corrective action.

When we come to see the universe in terms of connectedness rather than as a collection of isolated, separate entities, this view changes everything about how we live. Strong compassion for the suffering we see around us develops. That compassion will grow as surely as a baby struggles to stand up and walk.

It becomes clear that there is a sentient quality in the universe, an aware, compassionate force. The Chinese call it the Tao, in the West we label it God. It flows as it will. It's not something that humans can intellectually understand. Our attempts to use this force to obtain our own selfish desires are presumptuous. Experiencing this force is a goal in most religious traditions, and many people are convinced that they have had a direct experience of this energy.

In the Buddhist tradition this force is symbolized by Kwan Yin, the bodhisattva of compassion. Bodhisattvas are personifications of spiritually developed aspects of the human personality. Kwan Yin has one thousand hands and one thousand eyes, with which she perceives and alleviates the suffering of the world. We are those hands and eyes. Compassion manifests itself in this world through our individual actions whenever we let go of our personal worries and desires.

The form this compassionate energy takes, whether it involves holding sick babies in hospitals, trying to save other species from extinction, or any of a myriad of other activities, is up to the individual. As we come to understand our interconnectedness with all beings, our compassion will grow spontaneously. Then labels such as "right" or "wrong" are simply unnecessary. One simply tries to help in whatever circumstances arise.

The practice of endless compassionate action to the point that one burns up one's self-centered worldview is a powerful spiritual path. Those few who actually practice this way of life freely, without feelings of separation or superiority, are the saints of the world. Most of us aren't saints because we haven't yet healed ourselves. We haven't experienced this wholeness directly, as more than an idea. If we try to make a difference but end up burned out and frustrated, then we still have some work to do on ourselves. Attempting to function from a place of unconditional compassion is a good way to find out how whole we really are.

Trying to live this way doesn't mean being codependent, or allowing an exploitive situation to continue, or being a coward or a wimp. When somebody acts destructively, it is important to take action to contain the damage. We still act as we can to change things when we are able. However, we act out of a naturally arising sense of compassion rather than from a rigid view of right and wrong, or this versus that. We can also be aware of the pain that caused somebody to act destructively and not just get swept up in judgment or anger.

But putting this theory into practice wasn't possible that day. Whatever clarity or equanimity I thought I had achieved in Zen practice vanished in a cloud of steam. I fled to the forest, furious that people could still be so indifferent to the long-term consequences of their self-centered actions after years of environmental information in the media. I was even more furious over the personal disruption I was going to have to handle.

Life is a give-and-take affair. When we are asked to give something we happen to be comfortable with giving, or asked to do something we like to do anyway, we do it and feel good. The opportunity reinforces the ego and our desired positive self-image. Sooner or later, however, we will have to give something we really don't want to give. Usually something of ourselves—time, energy, intimacy— that we just aren't comfortable giving is required. If we can avoid it, we do—we just refuse. But sometimes the situation is such that we can't refuse. This environmental fight was one of those cases.

I didn't want to go through a lengthy campaign wrapped up in anger and tension. How could I take action in a way that would not sour my own peace of mind for the duration? If I was attempting to live in a helpful way, how could that attempt not be hindered when I engaged in conflict? How could I fight the fight with compassion rather than with anger?

If my actions served only to protect my self-centered goals, then suffering would surely increase; peace would be lost as a result of the conflict. If, however, the action I took was really for all sentient beings, including the developer, then maybe it would be possible to act compassionately and clearly, to remain in a peaceful place regardless of what arose.

In order to act clearly and peacefully, I had to pay careful attention to my own mind, watching it unblinkingly as it went through all its self-serving games. Doing this at a Zen retreat was hard enough. Could I do it now for real, like a Zen-trained samurai warrior?

After sitting in the millions-of-years-old longleaf pine ecosystem for an hour the situation began to come into perspective. I was upset because I was so attached to a given outcome in the upcoming fight. I had to win, not lose. Yet in the sweep of ecological time, in the context of the global environmental impact humans are causing, no one person can save or lose the planet. Winning and losing were just my opinions and preferences. Even if I fought and lost the upcoming battle, the planet would resolve these issues in its own way. To think otherwise was simply an ego trip. With that perspective, the fear, anger, and tension disappeared and I could relax. Relaxed, I'd fight better and have more energy for the battle with the developer rather than wasting it on the battle with myself.

A few days later a follow-up editorial commended this project, asserting that the development would protect, and enhance, the bay. A new day had dawned, and we could trust the developer to do the job right because he said he would.

The first step was to write a convincing, scientifically accurate statement of what a marina and golf course would do to the bay, and provide information on how to oppose the project, where to write and whom to call. The paper that had run the first stories agreed to run my essay as an opposing point of view on their op-ed page. I sent it to all the other regional papers as a letter to the editor and started to assemble lists for a direct mail campaign.

When the letter ran in Port St. Joe, the town beside the bay, the phone started ringing. A lot of residents were ready for war, they just wanted to know how to fight. Learning that was a big shock. Not too many years before, a proposal to buy and preserve the dunes and beaches that were now covered with condos had been shouted down by local opponents who wanted growth and development ahead of everything. Something had changed.

After several months of working in the community, what was happening became clearer. As the beaches were built up across the bay from the rural, working-class town, the local way of life began to change. Places that used to be open to hunting were suddenly somebody's backyard. Driving a pickup along the beach to fish and drink beer on a Saturday night was under assault by newly arrived condo owners. You weren't free anymore, the townspeople said, and it was all because of these rich newcomers in the condos. People who had never given protecting the environment a second thought suddenly wanted to save the grass beds.

One afternoon I was invited to give a talk at an area civic club. When the floor was opened to questions, the first came from a rather angry looking man.

"You make a good case against the marina, Dr. Rudloe, but there's something about you environmentalists that really bothers me. How can you people be so concerned about saving wild places when there's so much human suffering? Isn't a child more important than some endangered bird or turtle? People are dying of malaria, of starvation, suffering everywhere. Don't you care about that?"

"Of course I care about the suffering of a sick child," I answered slowly. "It's the essence of humanity to care about these things, to share the suffering in some way and then to act to relieve it in whatever way we can find. But there's a close connection between a lot of the suffering that humans experience today and the increasing bleakness of the landscape as we lose other species. Like populations of any other species that grow explosively for a while and exceed the carrying capacity of their environment, we will grow and grow until we exhaust our resources and then we'll crash. And as we do, unlike most other species, humans will take out a lot of other species with us. Butterflies, frogs, whales, uncounted numbers of other species, are disappearing from the earth now."

Everybody looked confused. There was silence. I tried again.

"More and more, all around the world, poverty and war, disease and suffering are coming from the loss and destruction of our natural resources—fertile topsoil, forests, the fish of the sea, and clean water. The consequences are not limited to what will happen to St. Joe Bay. This marina project is part of a global process of environmental decline, overpopulation, and increasing poverty. In America these relationships are still distant from each other, so it's a little hard to see."

The local minister came to my aid.

"I think what you are trying to say is that in order to have any hope of relieving that suffering, we must learn to preserve the integrity of the planet itself—we can no longer take it for granted. We must protect the essential life support systems of climate and soil, atmosphere and water so that we may still live. And we must preserve the beauty and grace of nature so that we may still wonder. Human well-being and protecting the environment aren't either-or. We have to do one to do the other.

"The problem is that there are too many of us," he continued, "and a lot of us take too much of the world's resources to support luxurious lifestyles. If we better understood our personal, individual relationship to a baby dying of diarrhea in a third world slum, or a crack baby screaming in a neonatal intensive care unit, we would also understand why and how to preserve endangered species. These are not competing needs, they are different aspects of the same problem—a lack of connectedness with ourselves and with other lives. It's fundamentally a spiritual problem," he concluded.

"Exactly, and if we don't make that connection, the situation will be controlled biologically," I added gratefully. "Sometimes there's a tendency to glorify nature, to spell it with a capital N. Or sometimes we dismiss it as a collection of raw materials to be exploited. Either view assumes that people are not part of the 'natural world.' Yet in our impact on everything else, we are one of the biggest actors in the present time on this particular planet.

"You know," I continued, "it's no coincidence that many professional scientists are becoming conservation activists. A few years ago, such advocacy was considered unprofessional, but that's changing. We love the planet in its beauty, we rejoice in the power of the human mind to comprehend its intricacy, but we see close up the unraveling that is occurring, and many of us are deeply frightened for the future and the suffering that is happening before our eyes."

Within six months the regulatory agencies that would have to permit the development project were buried in letters of opposition, many from scientists all over the country. The marina permit application was withdrawn before it could be officially denied, but the developer held on to the site. He could always try again later.

# The Fragrance
# of Gardenias

Right now, all this dashing and searching you're
doing—do you know what it is you're looking
for? It is vibrantly alive, yet has no root or
stem. You can't gather it up, you can't scatter it
to the winds. The more you search for it the
further away it gets. But don't search for it and
it's right before your eyes, its miraculous sound
always in your ears.

ZEN MASTER RINZAI

The next Zen retreat came at a really bad time. As a result of all the time I'd spent on the marina fight, work was too stacked up to take off for several weeks, and there were some very difficult issues in the pile. However, I went anyway, and as soon as I arrived there was the usual rush of joy at being in a Zen setting again. The beauty of the great oak tree in the garden, the candlelit meditation room at night and before dawn, the light of sunrise pouring in the east window, and the bright colors of the mid-morning sitting were all old and dear friends. By now the setting was also overlain with memories of all that had occurred in this place—all the past retreats and positive changes that had come out of insights and decisions made in this room over the last several years.

As usual, the great event of the retreat would be if nothing happened. If the mud finally settled, it might be possible to experience the mental states that come from a clear mind. But the only way this could happen was first to perceive the mud, examine the mud closely and realize its origins, as I'd been doing in all those previous retreats. It's an essential phase that cannot be skipped over. Eventually, however, as we resolve some of our difficulties, it may become possible to look beyond the personal movie. No one can be very helpful to others until he or she is practicing at a level more general than just dealing with personal problems.

No personal agenda at a retreat means you can begin to examine mind as a general phenomenon. The meditation room becomes a laboratory where one observes mental states—how they arise, their impact on the fundamentally simple activities of daily life, and how they complicate or enhance those activities. Not my mind, but the nature of mind.

We don't have a clear understanding of human mind and consciousness. We have myth, religious dogma, and philosophical speculation. Science has avoided the subject until recently because it lacks the tools to address it. We do know that we are the first species on this planet to manifest the mental complex of self-awareness, the technological ability to do things beyond our biological limits, the ability to imagine and project into the future, philosophical concern for ultimate meanings. We are also still aggressive and predatory when under sufficient stress.

Our brains relate past memory to present experience and then seek a preferred future outcome because natural selection favors that ability. Physical survival is enhanced when the organism uses a sense of self to direct its actions. But then the brain tries to protect the self and sees it as something with independent existence.

Dr. Ian Stevenson's work on past-life memories suggests that individual human mind and awareness can, at least sometimes, persist independently of the individual material body. Some psychic phenomena and the effectiveness of prayer are now documented in peer-reviewed scientific publications. These studies suggest that the mind can, in some circumstances, operate independently of the physical body and at a distance. And while something very like the near-death experience can be induced in the brain, that phenomenon has recently been demonstrated to occur spontaneously despite the absence of any measurable electrical activity in the physical brain.

Zen and other intensive meditation practices induce mental states that seem to be independent of material form and in a very different fabric of time-space or outside of time-space altogether. Some of these mental states are clearly associated with activity in the physical brain, but why are they encoded into the brain? Are they the gateway to a real nonmaterial awareness or are they only illusions that have been preserved by natural selection because they enhance an individual's material survival? People who think they understand their place in some eternal reality will be happier and more biologically fit than those who feel isolated psychologically. Is that all there is to it? The only answer seems to lie in experiencing the mental state and then deciding what to make of it.

For the first time, the long hours of sitting were relaxing and energizing, not just a strenuous grind. For once my mind was still and quiet rather than endlessly chattering to itself about the specifics of my situation. After a few days a sharp awareness of the nuances of each moment appeared—the weave of the cloth of a robe, the movement of wrists while rolling up the mat after breakfast, the shape of a hand holding a pencil, or the texture of the wooden table while writing a note.

The teacher at this retreat did a lot of teaching during the sitting periods.

"Look deeply into that which you love," he said in his initial talk. "That is where you will find the dharma, the Truth, as it is revealed in your life, your situation. Only give your body permission to actively love what it loves. Love is not complete without an active manifestation and expression of it in one's living actions, thoughts, and words.

"The only solution is to find your enlightenment in what you love and then to deepen it by asking, Why do I love it? Ask the right question in life—don't endlessly focus on the negative. Then hold up what you love, celebrate it, and share it endlessly with others."

The next morning I sat on the porch after bows listening as a dog barked and a dove called. The dog barked with no other thought than to bark; the dove cooed completely focused on its cooing. Only people are a jumble of conflicting thoughts and emotions. We've got these complex, big brains, but without some training we don't use them effectively most of the time. Mostly we're like little kids trying to drive a car down the highway—the outcome is predictable.

Meditation, explained the teacher in his next talk, is like walking along a steep, ice-covered ridge. On one side is a deep chasm of sleepiness, vagueness, spaced out–ness. On the other side is the vertical mountain face of thinking and obsessive preoccupation with one's personal situation, the mindless repeating of conversations, and the replaying of movie clips in which we are always the star. Either way we make no headway along the ridge. There was no doubt in my mind about the accuracy of his description. I'd been stuck on that mountain face for years.

"If you spend this time in Noble Silence, internally as well as externally, when the time comes to deal with your issues, you'll have that much more clarity from which to act. On the other hand, if you sit here obsessing about your problems, you'll just be that much more compulsive, grasping, and obsessive in how you deal with them," he said.

After several more days of stillness and freedom from verbal thinking, images began to arise, a sort of preverbal thinking in pictures, but the experience didn't last long. The following day, I once again started to obsess as usual about personal issues and immediately began saying a mantra, "Let it be okay, let it be okay." But that's a prayer that often isn't answered because it's just saying, "Let circumstances turn out according to my desire."

I had been very frustrated at having no opportunity to communicate with the teacher except in short, rushed interviews. How could he possibly evaluate where I was if he didn't know the details of what I was doing in Florida day by day? I was completely missing the point that my movie was not what the teacher was looking for; he was more interested in whether the student can see beyond that movie. There was no use referring to what was going on at home or anywhere other than that moment and place. If I couldn't present a clear mind there in the interview, then it probably didn't exist anywhere else. A calligraphy on the wall outside the meditation room said simply, "Without Situation/True Life," pointing to how life is when we let go of the personal movie.

As we chanted the morning bell chant the next morning, it was suddenly clear that the only aid one should request from the universe is the wisdom and courage to deal well with events as they arise. Things happen as a consequence of what has happened before them. The Buddhist concept of karma is most familiar to Westerners as the biblical statement "As ye sow, so shall ye reap."

The wisdom and courage that we need and seek arise automatically out of continued spiritual practice. Just do it regularly, and all the wisdom and compassion in the world will appear. My petition was responded to before I ever formulated it.

Sitting with physical struggles and a mind full of personal problems is exhausting, whereas calm, mentally quiet meditation is a source of rest, healing, and new energy. From clear, focused, alert meditation free from personal struggle comes joy, energy, and insight. The deeper the stillness, the more joy, energy, and insight there are.

I understood this clearly but still had trouble doing it, was still too preoccupied with my problems at home. At the next interview I asked, "Just try to stay mindful and in the present in each moment—is that all I need to be doing?"

"Yes," he said, "that's all it is. That's why hardly anybody masters Zen—it's too simple. The present is all there is anyway, right? Where else is there? There's no past and no future, and there's not really any present either.

"In spiritual practice," he continued, "there is the reception, the inhalation, the receiving and experiencing of simply what is in a complete way that has no separation. That partakes of limitless infinity—not a human pretending to be a bird but the true no separation of bird and human.

Inhaling, we experience our true nature. Exhaling, we manifest our true nature by taking action. Inhalation, exhalation, reception, presentation. All together, this equals love. Only when activities are totally engrossing in the present moment can they be clear practice."

That afternoon he told a story:

"Where will I go when I die?" asked a dying person.

"Wherever your toes lead you!" came the spare and frank response.

"This," the teacher said, "is faith that the universe is complete, whole and alive, and compassionate."

I suddenly realized that I had this faith concerning dying and might not be afraid when the time came. But if I really had faith in the moment of death and could go freely into that adventure, why didn't I have faith in the same force while living each moment? Why did I not bring that same confidence to whatever events marked the unfolding of this life? Why did I not just make my best effort and then peacefully leave the rest to the universe, trusting that everything is part of a whole, that we are a part of that whole, and that the totality is finally compassionate? Cherishing my opinion of how things should be, and trying to force events to happen as I wanted them to only proved that I didn't really have the experience that the entire universe is a shining whole and that we are safe regardless of events.

In the next moment, I knew that I could have faith in the process of death because death unfolds primarily independently of our will; we don't have to do anything about it. Dying is like being a passenger on a train. Daily life, by contrast, seems to be full of active choices and the task of deciding what to do next. We come to believe that outcomes will be determined by these choices. This belief is a heavy load to carry. Our choices, which are driven by our desires, do influence how circumstances develop, but the final outcome is not under our control. If we make our best effort, then our job is done. Whatever results after that isn't our failing or our victory. The rest of the outcome will play itself. With sufficient practice, we can relax and trust that each outcome is also part of one organic whole, from which we cannot be separated.

The next morning, chanting resonated energy. The sound was an act of opening to the universe to receive whatever it would send; it was a reaching out for connection. Afterward, we sat under the beautiful spreading oak tree just like Buddha had sat under the bo tree. It was obvious that perception is clearer outdoors than inside a building where the light is artificial and we are shut off from outdoor sounds. Outside was the original habitat where the human brain and mind evolved. A statue of the Buddha on the altar tells only half the story. According to Buddhist tradition, he was born under a tree, attained Enlightenment under a tree, died under a tree, always set up his camps in groves of trees.

The fragrance of gardenias filling the air, the rich chorus of birds, the people sitting, the early morning sunlight on the massive gray pine trunks, the oak canopy with its lacework of leaves, these gifts were enormous. They encompassed all of the galaxies above, and the DNA and quantum particles within. The entire complex appeared effortlessly, requiring no giver, no receiver. This was the matrix of which we are a contiguous part. We can respond to this fabric like fish to water if we are simply still for a while.

During the last sitting, I mentally chanted, and a solution to the difficult personal problems I'd been tussling with suddenly appeared. It wasn't very complicated. Several years of working on one project seven days a week at a level that had been exhausting suddenly became the practice of no separation, of total commitment to that work and place as a place of practice. If we ever keep a commitment to a way of life beyond the point of exhaustion, continuing on in a devoted rather than a neurotic way, we can experience no separation, only the flow of the task. Doing this means not keeping a certain distance. It means giving up all resistance and resentment and the very idea of exhaustion. No separation means no doubt, no fear, no frustrated desire for something else. We find exactly what we need in that situation. Then peace is possible, well-being is possible. Giving and receiving become one thing. When you become one with your problem, that's the solution to the problem.

Beyond continuing to do this in my work, it was clear that going to the forest and practicing meditation more intensely in the manner of the forest monks and nuns of ancient times was enormously important. I should begin to do this practice as soon as circumstances would allow me to without causing harm to those around me. If nothing resulted from my various professional projects, I would simply be closer to being able to practice at a monastic level and learn what that had to teach.

My needs in that respect were already taken care of; they were met with infinite generosity in my wilderness home. There I could practice outside and, if I stayed in that place, I would be able to go more deeply into Zen practice far sooner than if I were distracted with other projects. So I had an excellent option if my professional plans didn't work out. And, just like that, I was home, free and at peace.

The solution became clear in a flash, in a way that made words and thinking slow and clumsy. The fragrance of the gardenias was the fragrance of Kwan Yin, the bodhisattva of compassion, or Mary, or the Great Mother Goddess. She has a myriad of manifestations as situations demand, but this was her just now. This realization was the receiving of her infinite love, compassion, and help. It had taken me years of struggle to reach that point of surrender and wholeness, but now I was there.

The spiritual path usually has several stages. First there is struggle to achieve our desire, followed by growing pain as our efforts don't give lasting happiness (whether we get the immediate prize or not). Then we begin the attempt to confront the inadequacy of what we have been doing and find another way.

Eventually, when our aggressive efforts to fix the situation don't work, surrender of the ego comes together with an appeal for help in the form of chanting or prayer. This isn't an appeal that demands "Give me my desire," rather it creates an openness for whatever help might appear. It comes out of a deep sense of unknowing, an unknowing far larger than that created by any unanswered koan. It's accepting "thy will be done" for real.

This surrender of willful ego is a critical step. It is impossible for us to receive the help that is always available, it is impossible to receive the resolution of our cry, it is impossible to feel the love that is always there until we give up insisting that the world conform to our will, stop trying to force the situation to match our opinion, and cease to cherish our opinion at any cost, which only costs life itself. One must truly surrender will, opinion, and desire; one must let go of the branch, step off the thousand-foot pole.

Having finally done this, and it often takes years, we come to know that at the deepest level the events of life are there as the path to greater wisdom. We finally know that we are loved, sustained, and part of the whole. Our real needs—what we need to mature spiritually—are always met with the greatest generosity. We are not isolated, alone, and fearful. Only then can we trust in daily life as one can trust in the moment of death.

Finally there is expression of this resolution in one's life and work. The practice of repeated surrender, and appeal, and reception of help equals love, moment by moment, situation by situation. When stuck and miserable, just open up and let the dance arise, let the flowing of self and universe into each other happen.

If more people cultivated spiritual practice and got past struggle and surrender to resolution and manifestation, then a lot more love would be present in daily life. But, unfortunately, the early phases are the hardest ones to handle and many never get past them.

Life is not about being happy and whole because things worked out the way we wanted. Life is about being whole *regardless* of what happens. It's about a deep well-being that persists even though we might not be comfortable at the moment. This kind of peace is within reach of everyone, but it never occurs to most people that happiness can be based on anything besides getting what we want and being in pleasant external situations.

The insight that came out of the meditation period under the oak tree was that nothing else was necessary anymore for practice to be complete. Only ask how can I help in whatever the situation may be. Solutions to problems will develop at their own pace and only as they will. We must relax, slow down, and trust the resolution to occur as it needs to. Without a specific, rigid goal to struggle toward, we can be much more free, with much less struggle and pain and fear in the tasks we undertake.

Our place in this life, our only place, is wherever we find ourselves in each instant. An effort is made and results arise. The energy will go where the energy needs to go. The only thing to do is to live life without any resentment toward life and to pay attention to whatever teachers arise. Not only does energy flow *where* it needs to flow, independent of our ideas about it, but it also flows only *when* it needs to flow. We can't hurry the process; patience and trust are needed.

The results may or may not coincide with our notions of where we want the energy to go. Our idea of what an outcome should be is just our idea. It may or may not be in accord with what is going to happen. So long as we keep this in mind, we can deal with the results, regardless of whether they are what we might have preferred.

Even the frustration that arises so often is valuable. It's something to be pushed against and worked with, just like the artificial difficulties set up by a strict Zen retreat schedule. Pushing against the back pressure of frustration and working with it in a clear way builds strength. The role of any intractable problem is constantly to force us to give up over and over again the endless pursuit of desire. We must fall back on the only thing left, openness and trust in what simply is.

Life happens in the dynamic balance between frustration and success, and in finding the opportunities somehow to succeed in doing what needs to be done. And what needs to be done isn't at all about achieving some personal gain.

As for the circumstances of a single lifetime—whether one is successful or not, rich or poor, happy or lonely—that sort of personal karma is the product of the circumstances that are in momentary conjunction as that lifetime proceeds through its cycle. Environmental conditions, both external and genetic, shape and color a lifetime. They determine how life is expressed just as soil, water, temperature, rainfall, and competition from neighbors dictate whether a fruit will be rich and full or shriveled and small, or not even survive. The circumstances of a lifetime develop in accordance with the conditions in which it is lived.

Still sitting under the tree, I began to relax. What was this life all about? I still didn't know. It was eminently clear that the path of spiritual growth continued to stretch far ahead. Everything that had occurred in my life thus far was the merest beginning. Life is a perpetual unfolding with no end point. There is no place where I could say, "That's finished."

Evening sutra chanting came just before sunset. Golden sunlight poured into the room from the western windows, dancing on tiny dust motes in the air. As we sang, the dust particles seemed to rain gently down on our heads in a golden shower, like grace visibly descending. The sparrows that nested in the eaves of the porch were chattering and chirping for all they were worth. We sang louder and louder until we were belting it out with all our energy. The rafters were ringing, and suddenly the experience was transformed into one of those magic moments that soared on the sound. The intense awareness of the beauty of that moment equaled gratitude. The beauty, awareness, and gratitude all together are what made the magic happen.

The more the faculty of awareness is developed, the more gratitude appears and the more moments become magical. Desire and grasping had previously blocked this process nearly completely. Now the magic came from just singing 100 percent and not wanting anything more out of the experience.

When the world is luminous, there's nothing left to want. Everything is present; everything is complete. There's nothing to suppress or discipline. Being aware of this connection, knowing that everything is present, is all that is necessary. Life is complete.

The more we give, the more we receive. And the more we receive, the more we have to give, until there is no longer any distinction between giving and receiving. Nor is there anyone to give or receive. There is just a flow of energy continually blossoming anew and laughing and dancing as it does.

Then a mental image arose of an underwater sand fountain in a spring back in Florida. The water jetting out of a crack in the limestone kept the sand above it in a constant cascade. Endlessly cycling in its silvery plumes, the sand fountain had no beginning, no end, no going anywhere. There was just a perpetual moving round and round in a balanced, harmonious, and beautiful way. It was a model of the universe, and it was also a model of human existence. Each journey of a grain of sand up and down equaled a lifetime. Each grain's trajectory was determined by all the forces that were, or had been, or would be, present and acting on it. My life was one cycle of one of those sand grains.

Life is an iterative process, endlessly repeating the loop of finding a more correct situation, attaining more focus, experiencing more insight, and then using that insight to make the next situation in the next moment still more correct. And round and round and round life goes, endlessly merging into an ever-changing set of circumstances. From finding and living a balanced life to accessing focused mental states, to attaining insight from which comes compassion to once again achieve a further correct situation in the next moment is an endless cyclic process like the sand fountain in the spring. Before we die there are many iterations. It's not possible to resolve things with one answer for the rest of a lifetime.

Only when we stop running, accept our life as it has presented itself all along, only when we no longer struggle against life but work creatively within it can we begin to actualize our awareness in a concrete, living way. We can know what we truly are. From that place we can more readily attain the stillness in meditation from which further insight and clarity arise. Spiritual practice is alive and flowing, life is what it should be.

There is only whatever is happening at any given point in time. We continue the process of being aware of the cycling and remain in harmony with it day by day and moment by moment. When I first saw it, I had known immediately that the sand fountain in the spring was sacred, and now I understood why.

Life is a complex, ever-flowing, chaotic system. The experience of living is moving as a speck within the tumbling fluid flow, with currents and eddies coming from all directions. We can't control the flow, but sometimes an opportunity arises to move in the desired direction. When it does, move; when it doesn't, rest quietly but stay alert and in touch with the sources of energy. The specific details of how to move and what actions to take arise and disappear moment to moment, so vast flexibility is necessary. Having one concrete goal and a certain rigid path to achieve that goal rarely works. A vow and a direction are as much as one can realistically have in life.

At the most elementary level, there is no failure or possibility of failure in our lives. Each of us has a finite number of days to live. We don't know the number in advance, but on the last of these days we will die. This fact is equally true for every human being alive. We don't know what the circumstances of these days will be, but we do know we will experience and live them. All we have to do is live each day and then die as well as possible on the last one.

What is up to us is *how* we live each of the days, and how we react to whatever circumstances appear in them. Failure is impossible, but how we react is what makes the experience graceful or difficult. Some days are more painful, and some days are more joyous. We try our best in what we do but, having done that, we experience the day as it is. Regardless of whether the day turns out to be what we would have preferred, if we live it as well as possible, it is a day worth living.

Then chanting ended, the sun set, and we kept sitting under the stars. At the next interview, I tried to describe the entire experience to the teacher, but the effort was hopeless. The words only made layers of mud. He waited until I gave up the effort and then smiled. "Well, good! Retreat after retreat, you've just kept asking questions about why things are done the way they are, skating around on the surface. It sounds like you've finally quit trying to figure out Zen practice. It's about time."

"After all this time, I've just now learned to meditate. Now I just need to go do it."

"Better late than never—so go do it." He laughed and bowed, ending the interview. I walked back out to the cushion and sat down again.

# Letting Go

From ancient times wise people and sages have
often lived near water. When they live near
water they catch fish, catch human beings, and
catch the Way. For long these have been genuine
activities in water. Furthermore there is catching
the self, catching catching, being caught by
catching, and being caught by the way.

ZEN MASTER DOGEN

A sea fog had blown in, and the world was gray and still. Even the waves were tiny. Big pines stood elegantly silhouetted against the mist, and the little sparrows on the shore seemed to have outrageously big feet compared with their bodies. There was just the ringing vastness of fog, sea, and the edge of the North American continent.

Then the sun burned through the fog and lit up the wildflowers along the driveway to my house. Two herons patrolled the dock, and a porpoise passed just beyond the outermost pilings, following the rising tide into the bay. I was caught and suspended in awareness of the total perfection of that moment—nothing was missing, nothing was needed. The completeness of the universe was in each wave as it softly broke on the shore as well as in the interlaced pine branches against the sky.

There were no self-centered issues here of careers, money, or relationships—no ego, no emotion, none of the ideas that tend to dominate in offices and homes. This was a realm in which words were not needed. They couldn't possibly convey the experience, and in fact did not even exist. The egocentric, verbal thinking mind was simply gone.

It was what the Zen statement "open your mouth, already a mistake" really meant. When there are words, talking, and thinking, *this* cannot be experienced. The experience was what Zen Master Seung

Sahn calls the primary point—the moment before thinking and ego appear. Forest and sea are primary place. They are the physical realities that function utterly without human thought. This realm is indeed everywhere at each moment. Everything around us except the busy human mind functions spontaneously in the realm without words.

Every experience like this had appeared as a result of paying total attention to a moment that was full of light until the moment suddenly shimmered and opened up into something vast and transcendent. Experiencing it requires being totally present, with the mind not anywhere else in the world.

It's hard to touch one of these moments. Most of the time, our minds are too busy and complicated. The stars of our own movies, we usually perceive life as a swirl that flows around the central point of "me," of "I." As we constantly talk to ourselves, we create our self-image, and our very solid sense of who we are. This concept of the self, of "me" inside my skin dealing autonomously with the vast collection of other distinct and separate entities that make up the universe is the basis of who we think we are. The results of actions based on this assumption are predictable because they are how we have always lived. It feels right. This is the mind that governs our daily life.

We tend to lump similar moments together. We link them with some abstract concept like "sitting Zen," and then we think of them as one thing, something solid. And from that assumption, it follows that our sense of self is also something solid. In making this assumption, we ignore the evidence of our senses and miss what is really happening.

The Buddha's Second Noble Truth is that the source of suffering is the perception of separateness that comes directly from the strong sense of self or ego that each of us maintains. We believe that we are isolated individuals staring out through our eyes at a universe that is distinct from us, that we are born and die alone and that death may well mean extinction of what we are.

As we watch the mind in meditation, it becomes apparent that "I" is only the sum total of a brain, its thoughts, emotions, perceptions, and the mental habits it forms. It becomes obvious that the sense of self that has a certain name, a certain history, a certain social security number, is nothing solid. If we look carefully at this everyday mind, we will see how erratically it hops around, coming in and out of focus on what is happening in each moment. This mind is swept endlessly by emotions and reflexes from past events as well as by anticipation of future events.

The most impermanent things of all are the thoughts within our minds that constantly arise and disappear, yet we build our sense of self out of them. To rely on that untrained mind leaves us in big trouble when things don't go well and in even more trouble as our world changes at the end of life. Then, all that seemed so real and solid collapses.

Spend time around a stroke victim or somebody with Alzheimer's disease or someone who has suffered a major head trauma. It is totally obvious that our everyday self, our personality, who we think we are, are functions of mental activity in the brain. When the physical brain is damaged or overwhelmed with drugs, this personality dissolves. It follows that when the brain dies that personality is simply gone. It's a very scary notion, and most people refuse to get near it. If the familiar, everyday self is a mirage, what is left? Sometimes people decide that there's nothing else and are left with a sort of bleak despair. But this is just another of the mind's opinions. It only replaces one concept with another.

Beyond this unstable awareness, another form of mind exists. That mind is like the clear sky, and our ordinary mind is like the clouds that appear and disappear, come and go. Some days the sky is clear, some days it's cloudy, but all we have to do is go above the clouds and the clear sky is always there. Our skin isn't the real barrier that keeps us from experiencing this deeper mental state. The barrier is created by the thoughts we think and the ideas of reality that we build out of them.

We are most literally not separate and distinct beings in the material sense. Our physical existence is a continuous flow of matter into and out of our form. Not a single cell in our bodies is original. The physical interconnectedness of DNA, food webs, the organic and inorganic worlds, and our bodies is obvious to anyone who looks. Matter continually flows into the patterns we call our bodies, stays awhile, and then flows out, like a slow motion whirlwind. The only thing that is constant in an individual is the information stored in the genetic code, and it too changes as species evolve.

We are equally not separate from the flow of energy. Remove the steady input of the sun's energy to the planet, and we would quickly cease to exist. Energy is constantly pouring in and being burned up to maintain consciousness. At the subatomic scale, matter and energy aren't even separate anyway, just alternate forms of what may turn out to be the same thing.

The world's spiritual traditions all affirm that this material connectedness extends to the conscious mind. This human mind didn't come out of nowhere. Our thinking and the sense of self it creates ultimately arise out of the tendency of matter and energy to self-organize into more complex patterns. Energy and matter self-organize and create life, and natural selection then produces verbal intelligence, which in turn generates thoughts, feelings, perceptions, impulses, consciousness—the amalgamation of which we label as self. What we call ourself is only is a small piece of the endless output of intelligence from this vast natural process.

Perhaps the proper question is not "What is the meaning of my individual life?" Perhaps that is looking at the wrong scale. A better question might be "What is the meaning of the fact that matter organizes itself into complex patterns that eventually develop conscious self-awareness and mind?"

Furthermore, if self-aware mind can appear in matter at the level of an individual human being, it is possible that mind could also appear at other scales. This universe is fractal, and fractal systems are self-similar at all scales. It is therefore possible that mind could be a characteristic of the universe at a much larger scale than what we observe on the surface of this one planet.

It could be that just as mind arises out of self-organizing matter, what we call God and presume to understand is actually a form of transcendent Mind, an integral part of the self-organizing, self-aware universe that is not yet included in the current materialistic, scientific understanding of reality.

We can't touch life, we can only touch the matter that it animates, but life is clearly present. Likewise, as life arises out of matter, the cosmic, compassionate, sentient awareness that does respond to us arises out of life. Matter is concrete, life is more tenuous, and responsive Mind is more subtle still. But it is there and animates and governs living and nonliving alike.

There is currently no way to prove this assertion analytically or rationally, and there's no scientifically accepted evidence for mental relatedness. However, the reality of no separation can be directly experienced in a manner that will leave no doubt in the mind of the one who experiences it.

All things, events, entities, and objects flow into one another and cannot be separated. There is a strong awareness of being part of a larger whole that is universal and beyond the specific, individual self. That experience has been called interbeing; it's what Christian contemplatives refer to as God's presence and love. After some practice of meditation, we may start to experience transient flashes of it.

This form of awareness is untouched by change or by death. The physical senses and the rational, analytical intellect cannot access this condition because the mental rush of our thoughts and emotions keeps it deeply hidden. From time to time, however, we may have a momentary experience of this mind, of transcendence, triggered by a piece of music, a beautiful natural area, or the most ordinary event of daily life.

To prepare oneself to experience this mental state, one can contemplate no separation in each moment of daily life. Be consciously aware of how interbeing is expressed in each moment and in each setting. Always ask what is no separation in this moment, be it driving, eating, working, loving, running, whatever. Thus, moment by moment, we deepen our conscious awareness of the reality of interbeing and prepare the way for the physical experience of it.

The European philosopher Spinoza once said, "Whoso loveth God truly must not expect to be loved by Him in return." Why? Because it is simply not necessary to be loved in return. A need to be loved back means there is still a feeling of separation between self and other. The love serves as some kind of bridge between two different beings. When we lose the illusion of separation, then we truly experience love. Everything is complete just as it is. There is no need for a separate force to return anything, because nothing is lacking.

Things may feel very incomplete and painful for us. How do we get from where we are to where it is really not necessary to seek anything? Only when the struggle becomes overwhelming can we finally give up, at the deepest level, our efforts to control the situation. The seeker must go more and more deeply into the situation, and become so at one with that situation that the ego, the separate, struggling self who is fundamentally alone in an uncaring universe, simply disappears.

But so long as we struggle for what we think we don't have, we simply don't notice the wholeness. When we don't notice it, we can't access it or draw strength from it when extra strength is needed. As Spinoza's approximate contemporary Angelus Silesius commented, "God, whose love and joy are present everywhere, can't come to visit you unless you aren't there."

That's why Zen practice is often so physically demanding. It is designed to get us to the point where we let go of all our previously unquestioned assumptions about how life is, what we can tolerate, and what is too much.

Zen is concerned with transcending the essentially false perception of separation and a separate self. This is not accomplished just by faith or by thinking about the concept or by rationally analyzing it. In silent meditation, one attempts to dissolve the illusion of separation by consciously refraining from words, verbal thought, and the ego these create. To experience the cosmic directly, we must somehow momentarily let go of the details of our particular set of circumstances and let the still, impersonal reality underlying it come front and center in our awareness. Then the illusion of a separate, isolated self drops away fully and the reality of how the universe functions and our role within it become clear and apparent.

At mid-morning one day I sat at home, watching the sea beyond the window. A friend of many years had died just a few hours earlier when his fishing boat sank. The wind that was blowing so hard during the night had built cold waves that sank the boat at 4:00 A.M. The frigid water slowly drained his warmth and killed him as the sun rose. By 9:00 A.M. that wind had died, and the sea was once again calm and beautiful, looked exactly as it always looked. The sea was an impersonal force utterly untouched by the events of just a few moments before; it was a nonhuman reality in which cause and effect were instantaneous, clear, and unyielding.

The tide was running hard. Suddenly the flowing in and out of the tides of the sea—one of the many ancient, vast beyond human knowing processes of the universe—was identical with the inhalation and the exhalation of my breath which was also always there, always flowing in and out. That movement of breathing is simply the same pulsing of life that starts anew in every embryo—every fish's gills, every heart that begins to beat, every neuron that begins to fire as life appears once again.

In *no way* was this breath "mine" any more than the tide of the imperturbable sea was mine. It was the Tao always at hand that I could experience consciously as a physical reality, not just an intellectual concept, whenever I simply directed attention to the breath. Breathing was the entire vastness of Tao, as vast as the tides of the ocean or the orbiting of a galaxy, to be experienced intimately.

All of what I thought of as "me" or "mine" was no more "mine" than was the flowing in and out of the breath or the flowing of the tides of the sea that snuffed out my friend. In fact, the sea had destroyed nothing because, alive or dead, here or transformed into something we do not fully comprehend, nothing is ever lost. Nothing is ever parted from the vast, beautiful perfection of the universe that in that moment was manifest as sunlight glittering on a calm sea and the cries of fishing seabirds. The birds' elegant aerial dance gave life only by creating death, a reality that we also rarely see as it truly is.

And not only was the breath a universal phenomenon but so was the entire body. It was just the endless replaying of the ancient DNA tape, including the brain and the sense of self that is derived from and dependent on the brain.

Just like that there was nobody home—the sense of self was a hollow delusion. Experiencing this reality made it impossible ever again to overlook the intimate vastness that permeates everything. It's impossible to fall off this planet.

The ultimate source of all suffering is being ignorant of our true nature and identifying with this transient character who will so soon disappear. Suffering is cured by letting go of total identification with the specifics of one's situation, even while continuing to deal with it as well as possible. Personal identity is recognized as only a construct, or the sum total of thoughts, intentions, memories, and feelings. When that construct is dropped, the individual personality can cease to exist and remain nonexistent for as long as the mind remains still.

In any instant that we can really let go of thoughts and words and the total identification with the mental construct of self that they create, then the wraith of "Anne" or "Joe" or "Mary," and the suffering associated with that identification, disappears. The larger, transpersonal reality that was obscured by ego can become apparent. Become silent and you're just not there. When you aren't there, the entire living universe flows into the space that has opened up. If, in the next instant, "Jack" or "Harry" or "Joan" once again becomes mental reality, then all the suffering wrapped around that name also reappears, and peace is gone again. Start thinking, and you're back inside yourself just like usual.

In a long retreat, words, thoughts, and the sense of self that they create may fade as one comes to live in the world without words day in and day out. A mentally silent day can be a day off from the life of whoever we think we are, if we want it to be.

When the mind is truly and deeply still, then perception is altered. This altered form of perception emphasizes continuity, whereas ordinary thinking perception emphasizes differentiation. The sense of a separate self is seen as the mental construct that it actually is. One then lives in that awareness, acting appropriately in ever-changing circumstances.

The most basic question in spiritual practice is What am I? However, What am I? is not a question that can be answered once and for all, because what I am changes in each moment. Don't make some abstract idea and then try to conform to it. Instead, cultivate a state of fluid responsiveness. Asking the question anew in each moment is a technique to keep the mind focused on each instant as we live it, thereby living more fully. Moments of clarity arise from time to time, as do moments of reverting to a painful, solitary, ego-based state, so it's not an all or none, now you've finally got it sort of thing. It is because these are experiential states, not intellectual ideas, that Zen training emphasizes experience over thought and analysis.

One day at a retreat, we had been sitting for hours with loud rain hammering on the roof. When I went to bed that night, an air-conditioning unit that had been roaring directly outside the window suddenly stopped. The noise was replaced with the underlying silence of the night, and the sound of the crickets that had been there all along but hidden by the machine's noise. The noisy machine was the small self, with all its conscious mental uproar, while the night, the stillness, and the crickets were the true self underneath all that. Zen is simply a matter of turning off the noise.

# About the Author

Anne Rudloe lives, works, and practices Zen in Panacea, Florida, a very small town on the edge of a very big ocean. She and her husband, Jack, run the Gulf Specimen Marine Laboratory, an independent nonprofit environmental center and aquarium. She received her doctorate from Florida State University where she teaches courses on marine biology and environmental issues. She is a freelance writer, and her work has appeared in *National Geographic* magazine, *Smithsonian* magazine, and others. She has published numerous papers in scientific journals as well. She has been a columnist for Florida Public Radio and has written a regular newspaper column on Florida ecosystems. She began Zen practice in 1986 and is a student in the lineage of Zen Master Seung Sahn. "What am I?" is the most fundamental question in Zen. She is still working on that.